Love, Morals and the Feminists

By the same author

Women's Suffrage and Party Politics in Britain, 1866–1914, 1967
The Punch Book of Women's Rights, 1967

Love, Morals and the Feminists

Constance Rover, *M.Sc.(Econ.)*, *Ph.D(Lond.)*

Deputy Head of Department of Sociology and Law,
North-Western Polytechnic, London

LONDON ROUTLEDGE & KEGAN PAUL

First published 1970
by Routledge & Kegan Paul Limited
Broadway House, 68–74 Carter Lane
London E.C.4
Printed in Great Britain by
Butler & Tanner Ltd
Frome and London

ISBN 0 7100 6693 7

Contents

List of Illustrations

Acknowledgments

My thanks are due to the Governors and Principal of the North-Western Polytechnic, London, for sponsoring my research in the women's emancipation movement and to many friends and colleagues within the Polytechnic for help and encouragement. The skilled assistance provided by the North-Western Polytechnic Librarian and his staff has proved invaluable.

I am also indebted to the former Librarian of the Fawcett Library, Miss Vera Douie, O.B.E., and the present Librarian, Miss Mildred Surry, for their help.

This work originated from a suggestion by Michael Hurst of St John's College, Oxford, that I should write something further on the women's emancipation movement; his interest in the project I developed was an encouragement.

In a book such as this, where the object is to follow a train of thought rather than to reveal new source material, one necessarily draws heavily on the work of others. The studies I have drawn upon are, I hope and believe, revealed in the text and footnotes and I wish to express my thanks to the authors and publishers concerned.

I am most grateful to my friend, Mrs Helen Whittick, and her daughter, Mrs Gillian Pitt, for looking through my completed script – in the latter instance, for taking a sociological look – and for their suggestions. As the saying goes, the faults are my own;

one's well-founded apprehensions in this respect, however, are considerably lessened if one's work is found to be broadly acceptable by persons whose judgment one respects.

I must thank Mrs Freda Childs for the care she has shown in typing this work and, lastly but not least, my husband for assistance rendered in manifold ways.

Highgate, 1969   Constance Rover

I

Introduction to 'The Enemy'

The enemy faints not, nor faileth
And as things have been, they remain.

Arthur Hugh Clough

Most aspects of the women's emancipation movement permit of straightforward treatment because there was a campaign for a defined object such as the vote, property rights, admission to the professions and so on, but the relationship between feminism and sexual morality is a complex one involving many contrasts and contradictions. Early feminism was associated with the French Revolution and free love; the women's emancipation movement in England, which may be looked upon as dating from the 1850s until the First World War, was dominated by that sense of propriety and respectability which was the hallmark of the middle-classes during that period – so much so that some male opposition to the women's vote was based on the fear that women would impose strict moral standards upon society. Lord Pethick Lawrence has written in his autobiography, when describing the opposition to women's suffrage:

> In particular it was said . . . that on sex matters women were narrower and harder than men; and that if they were given power they would impose impossibly strict standards of morality, and endeavour to enforce them by penalties for non-observance.[1]

It may be contended, with reason, that the suffragettes were scarcely looked upon as models of respectability; this certainly applies to most of their activities but there was a streak of prudery in the

Pankhursts, and in the sphere of public morality, propaganda was concentrated on the wrongs suffered by women at the hands of men, not on demands for greater sexual freedom. The failure of the professional woman to claim emotional and sexual freedom was remarked upon by Emma Goldman, the Russo-Jewish-American anarchist, who was working as a nurse in 1905. She wrote of her patients:

> Most of the women claimed to be emancipated and independent,
> as indeed they were in the sense that they were earning their own
> living. But they paid for it by the suppression of the mainsprings
> of their own natures; fear of public opinion robbed them of love and
> intimate comradeship. It was pathetic to see how lonely they were,
> how starved for male affection, and how they craved children.
> Lacking the courage to tell the world to mind its own business, the
> emancipation of the women was frequently more of a tragedy than
> traditional marriage would have been.[2]

Another interesting aspect of the history of feminism is that Josephine Butler, who supported the civil rights of prostitutes and campaigned against the Contagious Diseases Acts, has emerged an official heroine of the women's movement while Annie Besant, the first woman to advocate birth control on a public platform, has not. Many reasons can be found for this; to take one, Josephine Butler was single-minded in her efforts while Annie Besant supported a variety of causes in her long lifetime; but few would deny that the modern woman's emancipation, such as it is, owes more to control over family size than to the campaign against the Contagious Diseases Acts (which provided a measure of state regulation of prostitution in certain garrison and sea-port towns). Annie Besant has her admirers but there is no mention of her in Ray Strachey's classic history of the women's movement,[3] nor in the recently published centenary work by Josephine Kamm.[4]

In tracing the interaction between feminism and the great moral problems of Victorian and modern times, such as divorce, prostitution and birth control, it became obvious that some leading feminists had been affected by their own personal situation; only the wearer knows where the shoe pinches and it is not surprising that some who fell foul of the marriage laws and conventional moral standards should wish for change. For this reason I discarded various provisional titles for this work, such as 'Feminism and Public Morality', in favour of 'Love, Morals and the Feminists', as it was borne upon me that the activities of the various participants in the developing story, such as John Stuart Mill, Annie Besant and Marie Stopes, had been affected by their personal attachments and disappointments. Readers who feel that they cannot stand too much of the love-life of the early feminists are advised to skip Chapters IV and V, resuming at 'Divorce and the Double Moral Standard'.

A difficulty in examining feminism and morality is to find a standard of judgment. One has to ask, what morality, which morality? Should it be the public morality of the period we are studying or could we consider 'progressive' any attitudes or developments pointing in the direction of present-day standards, which we are apt to consider more enlightened than those of our Victorian forebears? In anything so relative as morals, what right have we to judge Victorians and Edwardians by modern standards, even supposing we know what these are? As Dr Leach said in one of the 1967 Reith lectures:

> Moral rules are those which distinguish between good and bad behaviour, and the first point I want to make is that these rules are variable. Morality is specified by culture; what you ought to do depends on who you are and where you are. . . . The content of moral prohibitions varies wildly, not only as between one society and another, but even in the same society as between one social class and another or between one historical period and another. Breathing apart, it is difficult to think of any kind of human activity which has not, at one time or another, been considered wrong.[5]

It is possible to look at the interaction between feminism and morality from several standpoints. One is the biological one, usefully defined by Desmond Morris in *The Naked Ape*:

> If certain sexual patterns interfere with reproductive success, then they can genuinely be referred to as biologically unsound. Such groups as monks, nuns, long-term spinsters and bachelors and permanent homosexuals are all, in a reproductive sense, aberrant. . . . The biological morality that I have outlined above ceases to apply under conditions of population overcrowding. When this occurs the rules become reversed.[6]

Should it be possible to show that feminism has contributed towards small family size, for instance, one might look upon it as immoral in periods of underpopulation and moral in the reverse conditions. The *Report of the Royal Commission on Population* (June 1949)[7] suggested that there was a connection between the fall in the birth-rate and feminism but J. A. and Olive Banks have provided evidence to the contrary.[8] Another point of view would be to look upon the development and happiness of the individual human being as the standard of value and to consider whether the impact of the contemporary public morality upon the feminist movement contributed to or detracted from this. A third possibility is to beg the question so far as feminism is concerned and consider it a valuable movement contributing to the expansion of opportunities for women and then to see to what extent prevailing moral codes helped or hindered this development. On the whole, the view has been taken that trends in the direction of modern, more liberal standards have been good.

The whole question of morality is, of course, complicated by its association with property and religion. Property and its inheritance are, for obvious reasons, basic to the double moral standard; Christianity, in spite of benefiting women through fostering respect for the individual human soul, has produced the image of an essentially masculine God, presumably countenancing the views of St Paul about women (though these may have been mistranslated or misinterpreted). One has a certain sympathy with the suffragette who encouraged a friend by saying, 'Trust in God; She will protect you!'

The essence of the matter, however, is that, in a sense, public morality (taken in its narrowest interpretation as relating to matters of sex) was the enemy of feminism. So long as women were judged solely on whether they conformed to accepted moral standards other qualities of personality or intellect being more or less irrelevant, they had no real hope of emancipation or equality. Men have always accepted the fact that it would be impossible to do business if an inquisition into private morals needed to be held before any negotiations could take place and although, in politics, a surface respectability has usually been required, quite a lot of private irregularity has been overlooked so long as open scandal could be avoided. This is not to suggest that licentiousness is desirable but that there are many other human qualities, apart from conventional respectability, which are rightly valued amongst men. The recent scandals known as the Profumo Affair have inspired reflections from A. J. P. Taylor and others to the effect that we do not judge the value of former prime ministers, such as Melbourne, Disraeli, Palmerston and Lloyd George, by the standard of their private morality. Even in the case of Jack Profumo, it was his deception of the House of Commons, rather than his private conduct, which was considered to be his cardinal sin.

The need to develop standards of value for women, other than 'respectability', has bedevilled the feminist movement and led to a situation where, perhaps, women have been their own worst enemies. A sort of *impasse* developed; to ignore conventional public morality was to invite and attract censure in a way which harmed efforts to obtain education, wider opportunities for employment, and so on, yet not to attack 'the enemy' was to perpetuate a situation where women were valued (or undervalued) for little other than their function as wives and mothers. Also, the nature of the enemy was not always understood. It was not the necessity for some sort of moral code which needed to be attacked but the attitude that conventional morality was the only thing that mattered so far as a woman was concerned and that this was a sphere in which no woman could be allowed any freedom, if she were to retain social approval. Just as feminists today argue that all restrictions on women's employment should be removed, even though they do not, for instance, envisage women wanting to be steel-workers, it is necessary for women to have freedom of person and freedom from what used to be the dead-weight of conventional morality, if emancipation is to be claimed, whether advantage is taken of such freedom or not. The 'Respectable Social System', according to Peter Cominos,[9] robbed the Victorian gentleman of spontaneity and emotional satisfaction, frustrating his creative potential; how much more repressive was its effect upon women.

That any seeming or actual attack upon the role of women as wives and mothers should arouse opposition from women as well as men is understandable. Everyone needs to feel his or her life is of some value and the importance of proper care for children is obvious; the implied suggestion, inherent in feminism, that the role of wife and mother is not enough and that a woman should have some sort of public life as well, aroused antagonism and still does so.

The battle goes on; the support given by religion to the conventional roles of the sexes has diminished along with the decline in religious belief, but to some extent its place has been taken by Freudian ideas supporting (or thought to be supporting) the thesis that women find fulfilment only as wives and mothers. And, of course, it is true that few women would wish to live without these experiences, but is this the whole truth?

What could be the most exciting chapter in the story of the interaction between feminism and morality will necessarily remain currently unwritten, for it belongs to the future. Now, in the second half of the twentieth century, the hold of Victorian prudery upon the British people and other Protestant communities has obviously been broken; the long-term effect of this upon the position of women is at present incalculable, but is bound to be immense.

Notes

1 Pethick Lawrence, F. W., *Fate Has Been Kind*, 1943, 68.
2 Goldman, Emma, *Living My Life*, 1932, i. 371.
3 Strachey, Ray, *The Cause*, 1928.
4 Kamm, Josephine, *Rapiers and Battleaxes*, 1966.
5 *The Listener*, 7.12.1967, 749, col. 3.
6 Morris, Desmond, *The Naked Ape*, 1967, 98–9.
7 H.M.S.O., *Report of the Royal Commission on Population*, 1949, Cmd. 7695.
8 Banks, J. A. and Olive, *Feminism and Family Planning in Victorian England*, 1964.
9 Cominos, Peter, 'Late-Victorian Sexual Respectability and the Social System', in *International Review of Social History*, 1963, viii. 18–48, 216–50.

2

France, Feminism and Free Love

'Lieben Sie treu?'
    'Nein, aber oft.'

Laube

The French Revolution produced the first combined effort made by women to attain citizenship in the period which we look upon as 'modern history'. Condorcet had been writing on the political rights of women, using arguments which in many ways foreshadowed those of John Stuart Mill; feminists such as Olympe de Gouges pressed the claims of their sex, and women's clubs were part of the 'club mania' of the period immediately following 1789. For a time, feminist activities formed part of women's participation in the French Revolution, but the period was short-lived and came to an end with the closure of the women's clubs by the Convention in October 1793.

Condorcet is credited with the first essay on the political rights of women.[1] This essay made a very moderate claim for women's enfranchisement using arguments which, though hackneyed today, were far in advance of his time. He tried to refute the anti-feminist claim that men were governed by reason and women by emotion. We are rather tired of this line of argument today and are inclined to suspect the rationality of either sex, but during the nineteenth century it was repeated endlessly. Condorcet was concerned to support the rationality of women, perceptively pointing out:

> Their [women's] interests not being the same [as those of men] by the fault of the law, the same things not having the same importance

7

for them as for men, they may, without failing in rational conduct, govern themselves by different principles, and tend towards a different result.[2]

If one eliminates the words, 'by the fault of the law', the idea expressed is applicable today and interpretative of many situations giving rise to misunderstanding between the sexes.

The egalitarian ideals of pre-Revolutionary writers paved the way for a feminist movement; support for goals such as political rights, individualism and liberty contributed to an intellectual climate in which some could not fail to extend the idea of the 'Rights of Man' to those of woman. Montesquieu, Voltaire, even Rousseau, all contributed their share by their support of political rights.

Women's activity at the time of the Revolution was part of the Revolution itself. The march of the market-women to Versailles was essentially a hunger-march, not a feminist protest. For women, as for men, the storming of the Bastille was symbolic of an end to tyranny. Men and women alike demanded the 'Rights of the People', and an end to aristocratic privilege. A minority of revolutionary women espoused the cause of feminism, prominent amongst them being Olympe de Gouges, Etta Palme von Ælders, Claire Lacombe and Théroigne de Méricourt. A limited measure of support was obtained from men, many of them being somewhat unrevolutionary in their attitude towards women and holding that wives should be at home looking after their families.

Divorce became permissible during the Revolution and both sexes took advantage of the fact. As might be expected, religion was a casualty of the times. The Goddess of Reason was enthroned in Paris and in certain provincial areas and some marriages were entered into without any ceremony other than a public declaration. The easing of the marriage laws did not last long and divorce was abolished by Louis XVIII on the restoration of the monarchy.

Perhaps the only permanent gain made by women during the Revolution was the inheritance law which provided that fathers should leave their estates to their children, female equally with male. Politically, women were worse off than before, as they had lost the limited feudal rights which a few of them possessed; nevertheless, the Revolution had shown it was possible for women to come out of the home and adopt a variety of roles, even that of the soldier.

One French writer surviving the Revolution, the feminist element in whose thought was (to put it mildly!) eclipsed by other aspects, was the notorious Marquis de Sade. He considered the position of women unfair both sexually and legally and demanded their complete equality with men. One of his biographers, Guillaume Apollinaire, considered that he gave his works, *Justine* (1791) and *Juliette* (1792), heroines rather than heroes to illustrate this theme.[3] In *La Philosophie dans la Boudoir* (1795) he contended:

> The right can never be given to one sex to take possession of the other; and never can one of the sexes or classes have an arbitrary right over the other.[4]

In view of the widespread prohibition of such of de Sade's writings as survived and the concentration of attention upon the erotic element in his work, it is doubtful whether his feminist ideas had any influence. In any case, any effect they had was bound to discredit the cause of feminism, as the mad Marquis was anathema to all right-minded people. Unacceptable to his contemporaries, de Sade's ideas became even more repugnant as the nineteenth century progressed and Victorian prudery descended upon the English, casting its shadow across the Channel. The idea of respectable family life, so dear to the Victorians and exemplified by the Queen and her consort, had been deplored by de Sade, who saw in the family group the greatest danger to equality and to the state, considering family interests anti-social. He advocated the establishment of national schools for the upbringing of all children, to avoid the inconvenience occasioned by their rearing.

The idea of free love is more specifically associated with the Saint-Simonians than with the French Revolution. The writings of Claude-Henri de Rouvroy, Comte de Saint-Simon (1760–1825), included an interpretation of history and ideas leading towards positivism, socialism and a new religion. He was not basically feminist and it seems possible that his sole direct contribution to the theme was made to please Madame de Staël, to whom he made an unsuccessful proposal of marriage. This contribution took the form of a bizarre new religion, centred round Newton, which held that the law of gravitation was the great unifying principle of the universe. A subscription was to be opened at Newton's tomb, contributors were to vote for the Council of Newton which would govern the world, women could subscribe and therefore vote and they could also be nominated for the Council.

Saint-Simon was seldom satisfied for long with any one scheme and soon lost his attachment to the law of gravitation. A somewhat more basic feature of his thought was his belief that history was divided into cycles of critical or destructive phases alternating with constructive epochs. He looked upon the eighteenth century as a critical epoch destroying traditional religion and sought a new creed which would fulfil the needs of the constructive era which was dawning and in which the whole of society would strive towards the amelioration of the poorest class. Finding Christianity unsatisfactory, he developed, at the end of his life, his *Nouveau Christianisme* (1825). The golden age, Saint-Simon claimed, was ahead, not in the past. The idea of the fall of man was erroneous, the doctrine of progress prevailed and this would eventually lead to an earthly paradise. It followed that the Christian idea of the mortification of the flesh to expiate original sin was wrong and should be discarded. Physical well-being and happiness were desirable, as well as moral elevation. Had Saint-Simon survived 1825 he would no doubt have developed fresh ideas superseding his *Nouveau Christianisme*, but as it was, his followers took up and developed his theme to the logical conclusion of the 'rehabilitation of the flesh', which was central to the belief of the Saint-Simonian school. They realized too that the new religion could not be called Christianity.

Perhaps the most important of the adherents to Saint-Simonism was Barthélémy Prosper Enfantin (1796-1864), who considered that free love was legitimate in a collectivist society and that it should replace marriage for those who found the institution tyrannical. He also supported the emancipation of women.

The Saint-Simonian religion had considerable influence in Germany and became tied up with the Young German movement, which also advocated a measure of feminism and socialism. The literature of the movement included somewhat uncertain attacks on Christianity and the marriage laws, which led to the suppression of the Young Germans and their works by Federal and Prussian Edicts. The reactionary establishment which sensed a dangerous revolutionary conspiracy in the relatively harmless activities of the

Young Germans has given to some of the banned works a scarcely deserved importance.

The 'rehabilitation of the senses' led to the romantic movement in literature in both France and Germany. The novelist Georges Sand (1804–1876) was in sympathy with Saint-Simonian ideas and was a notable example of an emancipated woman who maintained herself (and at times her lovers) by her own efforts, wore men's clothes when she felt like it and was prepared to live in defiance of conventional society. She was also serious-minded, hard-working and frequently long-suffering so far as her friends and relations were concerned. Her *Lélia* (1833) is critical of society and the marriage laws and her earlier novel, *Indiana* (1832), shows strong Saint-Simonist influence.

Reading the annals of the times, one is tempted to think that a doctrine of free love was scarcely necessary in France. (The French have a similar opinion of English society.) But there is a great difference between paying lip-service in public to conventional religious and moral precepts, while ignoring them to a certain extent in private, and openly challenging these precepts. The latter could be a threat to the whole fabric of society, as the Revolution had shown. Religion and morals were the cement of society and when attacks on them were associated with socialist ideas and suggestions for changes in the position of women, there was every reason for antagonism from those profiting from the existing state of affairs. This association between the revolutionary French, free love and feminism caused the concept of feminism to be abhorred across the Channel, where the English were in any event not predisposed towards it. Nevertheless, Saint-Simonian missionaries came to England in 1832 and were assailed by the anti-socialists jointly with the Owenites. The noted feminist Anna Wheeler formed a link between the Saint-Simonians in France and the English Co-operators (see Chapter 4). Missionaries also penetrated the U.S.A.

From the time of the French Revolution, there was no further organized effort by women to improve their position until the Anglo-Saxons took up the theme of 'women's rights' in the mid-nineteenth century. In the U.S.A. a local convention on women's rights was held in 1848 at Senaca Falls and a national convention at Worcester, Massachusetts, in 1850. In Britain, although there had been earlier activity in some directions, a continuous campaign may be said to have started in the 1850s with the organization for married women's property rights.

An interesting contrast emerges between the women involved in the early French outbreak of feminism and the later Anglo-Saxon movement. The Frenchwomen, in spite of their women's clubs, were mainly individualists and lacked that sense of sex solidarity which distinguished the members of the English and American societies; many of the French leaders were unashamedly 'men's women' and some, like Théroigne de Méricourt, ex-courtesans. The Englishwomen, in spite of holding what passed for advanced radical views, bore the stamp of middle-class respectability, as did most of the Americans with some exceptions such as Victoria Woodhull. If one ignores the female hooligans thrown up by the French Revolution from the lowest quarters of Paris, continental feminists tended to be of a bohemian type, particularly those associated with the Saint-Simonian movement; in England there were a few individualists, such as Mary Wollstonecraft, who were prepared to flout convention, but the organized movement of the second half of the nineteenth century bore an unmistakable bourgeois stamp.

Much more could be said and many more well-known names mentioned in connection with the French Revolution, the Saint-Simonian movement and early feminism, but sufficient has, perhaps, been outlined to indicate that early feminism was closely identified with a new definition of sexual morality, perhaps even more closely than with the demand for an improved legal and civil status for women.

Notes

1 Condorcet, 'Sur l'admission des femmes au droit de Cité', in *La Société de 1789*, 1790.
2 Translation by Dr Alice Drysdale Vickery.
3 Gorer, Geoffrey, *The Life and Ideas of the Marquis de Sade*, 1953, 1962 reprint, 130.
4 De Beauvoir, Simone (trans. Paul Dinnage), *The Marquis de Sade*, 1962, 135.

3

England and Early Feminism

See Wollstonecraft, whom no decorum checks,
Arise, the intrepid champion of her sex.

Richard Polwhele (1798)

In England the climate of opinion was particularly unfavourable
to feminism during the late eighteenth and early nineteenth centur-
ies, owing to the excesses of the French Revolution and England's
sufferings during the Napoleonic wars. The feeling was that the
French were bad, revolution was bad, the French Revolution had
led to feminism, therefore feminism must be bad. A somewhat
similar association of ideas affected radical thought and there was
an oppressive, conservative, political reaction which lasted until
1822, after which the Tories turned to reform in place of repression
and the harshness of the regime was slowly mitigated.

During the period between the French Revolution and the development of an organized women's movement in the 1850s, there
were some unorganized feminists, held in varying measures of
esteem and disrepute, who did not follow the prevailing code of
public morality. This was in part coincidental, in that they happened
to fall in love with the 'wrong' person and in part due to the fact
that people with 'advanced' views and the courage to support unpopular causes, such as feminism, the 'new philosophy', freedom of
the press, deism, atheism, radicalism and socialism, were likely to
have the courage to challenge conventional moral standards. Practically all were serious-minded and we know of them because they
made their mark in literary circles and through their support of
various progressive causes. They did not all feel as strongly as John

Stuart Mill (whose activities extended from this early period into the main period of the women's emancipation movement) on the evils of the subjection of women and the iniquities of the marriage laws.

Most historians of English feminism tend to start with Mary Wollstonecraft's *Vindication of the Rights of Woman*, published in 1792. This is looked upon as the first important woman's protest against the degraded position of her sex. She concentrated particularly on the need for education, so that women's reasoning faculties could be developed to render them better able to fulfil their duties as wives and mothers. She was concerned with the substance rather than the form of marriage and was anxious that it should become more meaningful. This she held would only be possible if women were capable of giving intelligent companionship to their husbands and sound, moral training to their children. As governess to Lady Kingsborough, she had become disgusted with the shallowness of society life and what she considered to be the neglect of their children by society women. Her *Vindication* was published before there was any irregularity in her personal life but her subsequent love-life inevitably augmented the association in the public mind between feminism and immorality. Also, her views on marriage developed to the stage where she came to believe that mutual love between a man and a woman constituted marriage and that the parties to a union should not consider themselves bound to each other after the death of love.

Mary Wollstonecraft's concern for the substance rather than the form of marriage relationship led her to a situation where she found herself without either. In a sense, her difficulties stemmed from her being all too normal, physically and emotionally. Her friendship with the Swiss painter, Fuseli (then working in England), seems to have aroused her emotions. Fuseli was married and Mary appears to have been surprised to find that she could not carry on a high-minded Platonic friendship with him without distress. In her *Thoughts on the Education of Daughters* (1787) she had written, 'Nothing can more tend to destroy peace of mind, than Platonic attachments'[1] and she found it all too true. At the end of 1892, she deemed it advisable to put some distance between Fuseli and herself by going to France, even though her arrangements to go there with friends fell through. She eventually went alone, and here, in her loneliness, she met Gilbert Imlay, an American, attributing to him (by a process of wishful thinking) high-minded qualities which he did not possess. There seems little doubt that she looked upon herself as married to him, although no ceremony took place and, indeed, could not at the time their association commenced, as it would have involved Mary in difficulties with the French authorities through the disclosure of her British nationality. Her distress, when Imlay eventually deserted her and the child she had borne him, was all the more acute on account of her high ideals and led her to attempt suicide.

Mary's subsequent attachment to William Godwin, the philosopher, was again without benefit of clergy at first, though they had sense enough to marry when a child was expected. Godwin was on record as disapproving of marriage, feeling that young people should not make binding contracts for life in ignorance of whether they would wish to be held to them in years to come. In his *Memoirs of Mary Wollstonecraft* (1798) he wrote of their early decision to unite without marriage:

> For myself, it is certain that I had for many years regarded marriage with so well-grounded an apprehension, that, notwithstanding the partiality for Mary that had taken possession of my soul, I should have felt it very difficult, at least in the present stage of our intercourse, to have resolved on such a measure.[2]

In Mary's case, her initial reluctance to enter into a permanent union seems to have been an instance of once bitten, twice shy after her disastrous affair with Imlay. Her short married life went well, although, to her surprise, many of her friends turned against her on the announcement of her marriage to Godwin, for they could no longer deceive themselves as to the nature of her previous union with Imlay.

Mary Wollstonecraft's orginality of thought shows up in marked contrast to that of her contemporary, Hannah More, who also wrote and worked to improve the state of society but who did not seek to question convention. Hannah More took the current social order for granted, including its class distinctions, but believed the poor should lead a more religious life in the station to which they had been called. She and the other blue-stocking ladies, though not feminists,

contributed towards the raising of the status of women by maintaining standards of personal excellence and making it obvious that some
women had qualities of mind and character which could elevate
social life.

One might have thought, in view of his philosophy, that William
Godwin would have taken up the torch which his wife had set
alight, but he was no believer in sex equality. As he put it in his
essay 'Of Love and Friendship', 'Nothing can be more certain . . .
than the inequality of the sexes.'[3] Godwin believed that man's
unfortunate condition was the result of a bad environment, in
particular bad government, but that it was possible for the environment to be changed and life improved; in short, he believed in
progress and human perfectibility. This belief, common to the
supporters of the 'new philosophy', that character was stunted and
distorted through bad environment, coupled with a disbelief in
innate characteristics, had an obvious application to women. In the
male environment it was at least thought desirable that some attempt
should be made to show good sense, strength and knowledge, but
women were trained to give an appearance of frailty, ignorance and,
often, frivolity. If this inferior female character were the result of
bad training, then it was not based on any innate inferiority and
could be changed. Though many did not trouble to make the connection between the new thought and the position of women, the
logic was obvious to those who chose to look.

Mary Wollstonecraft was derided by her contemporaries and
many of her successors. In Horace Walpole's oft-repeated phrase,
she was a 'hyena in petticoats'. Her admiration for the French
Revolution was held against her and no abuse was too bad for a
Jacobin. The charges against her included immodesty, because she
was interested in botany, and indecency, because she advocated
athletics for women. The elopement in 1797 of her former pupil,
Mary Elizabeth King, and the subsequent scandal were attributed
to Mary Wollstonecraft having been her governess ten years
earlier. Most unfairly, the lives of Fanny Imlay and Mary Godwin,
as Mary Wollstonecraft's two daughters were called, were taken as
examples of her baleful influence. The two girls were treated un-
kindly by their stepmother, the former Mrs Clairmont, whom Godwin married in 1801. At the age of twenty-two, Fanny committed

suicide. Mary Godwin, at seventeen, eloped with the poet Shelley, accompanied somewhat surprisingly by her stepsister, Jane (Claire) Clairmont. Mary Godwin and Shelley were married after Shelley's estranged first wife, Harriet Westbrook, had also taken her own life. These events cast discredit on the family, although Godwin played the role of conventional father, banning Shelley from his house when the attachment between the poet and Mary became apparent and trying to effect a reconciliation between Shelley and Harriet. The marriage between Mary Godwin and Shelley endured until the latter's untimely death and Mary (the author of *Franken-stein* at nineteen) lived down her past and became a respected literary figure. If any woman (other than the girls involved) need be blamed for these events, it would have to be Godwin's second wife, who seems to have doted on the daughter of her first husband, Jane (or Claire, as she preferred to be called), at the expense of her step-daughters and who, from all accounts, was a thoroughly conven-tional, 'womanly' woman. The devotion lavished on Claire apparently did her no good, for she fell in love with Byron at seventeen, with disastrous results. It was obviously unfair to blame Mary Wollstone-craft for events which happened long after her death, but the know-ledge that she had twice attempted suicide and had had an irregular association, first with Imlay, then with Godwin, was added to the subsequent family history to discredit the pioneer feminist.

It is quite impossible to read Mary Wollstonecraft's works with-out concluding that all her literary influence was on the side of virtue. Her claim for rights was always coupled with the acceptance of duties; indeed, the claim was based on the need for a situation for women, so that they could better perform their duties and 'ad-vance, instead of retarding, the progress of those glorious principles that give a substance to morality'.[4] In her Dedication of the *Vindica-tion* to Talleyrand, late Bishop of Autun, she makes an honest, straightforward claim for women's rights, not hedged about, as so many subsequent claims have been, with qualifications intended to make it clear that women would not default in their traditional domestic duties.

> If the abstract rights of man will bear discussion and explanation, those of woman, by a parity of reasoning, will not shrink from the same test. . . .

Consider – I address you as a legislator – whether, when men contend for their freedom and to be allowed to judge for themselves respecting their own happiness, it be not inconsistent and unjust to subjugate women, even though you firmly believe that you are acting in the manner best calculated to promote their happiness? Who made man the exclusive judge, if woman partake with him the gift of reason?[5]

What modern feminist, however militant, could improve upon this last sentence? The memory of Mary Wollstonecraft now seems fully rehabilitated, and she appears to have achieved a worldwide reputation. As well as the learned theses concerning her which have emanated from Europe and the U.S.A., she is apparently known in the Far East. In 1959 the British Museum informed the Fawcett Society (London) that an enquiry had been received from Japan asking what was being done to celebrate the bicentenary of Mary Wollstonecraft's birth. The Society's distinguished librarian, Miss Vera Douie, O.B.E. (now retired), told the writer that at the time it had not occurred to them to do anything at all but they hurriedly decided to make appropriate arrangements, staging an exhibition at Fawcett House and a ceremony at St Pancras Old Church, when a wreath was laid upon Mary Wollstonecraft's tombstone.

Mary Wollstonecraft's life was one of struggle and effort. At a time when it was difficult for a woman to be independent, she maintained herself and, frequently, her relations, by her own endeavours. The fact that in her personal life she had the courage to live by her convictions only adds to her stature.

The parity between the views on marriage held by Mary Wollstonecraft and Godwin and the law in Russia today is interesting. Apparently a divorce may be obtained in Russia if the parties declare they no longer love one another and that the marriage has failed, though an attempt at reconciliation must be made before the divorce is granted. In the absence of children, there is no difficulty whatever and when there are children, a certain fixed percentage of income is paid to the parent looking after the children by the other parent. There also seems to be a move afoot to simplify the procedure still further by making it possible to register the dissolution of marriage without the necessity of going to court. Maintenance and alimony do not form part of the system, excepting that an incapacitated, divorced person may be maintained for a maximum of one year from the date of the divorce.

Obviously such a system is viable only if women can be expected to support themselves and the Russian assumption is that all able-bodied adults of suitable age should work, mothers receiving considerable help from social services.

Whatever one's views on the Russian way of life, no one would claim that it has led to an atmosphere of gay debauchery. On the contrary, to Western eyes, the Russians appear serious to the point of dullness and the general atmosphere seems puritanical; the Russians themselves make no secret of their disapproval of the 'decadence' of the West. One cannot help feeling that there is much in the modern Soviet system of which the serious-minded and, indeed, somewhat humourless Mary Wollstonecraft would have approved.

Notes

1 Wollstonecraft, Mary, *Thoughts on the Education of Daughters*, 1787, 88.

2 Godwin, William, *Memoir of Mary Wollstonecraft*, 1798, 1928 edition, 103.

3 Godwin, William, 'Of Love and Friendship', in *Thoughts on Man*, 1831, xv, 292.

4 Wollstonecraft, Mary, Dedication in *Vindication of the Rights of Woman*, 1792, ix.

5 *Ibid.*, ix–x.

4

The Early Feminists and the Marriage Laws

Chastity, sexual intercourse with affection.
Prostitution, sexual intercourse without affection.

Robert Owen

In any occupational or social group one could find a number of unhappy or broken marriages and a catalogue of these drawn from the feminists would be pointless if it were not that the course of feminism has been affected by the personal circumstances of those involved. Moreover the activities of some of the pioneers impinged upon the great moral issues of Victorian times, such as divorce, birth control and 'the great social evil', as prostitution was termed. One does not wish to rehash the lives of feminists which have already been well described and documented – in particular, it would be presumptuous to try to add anything to recent publications concerning John Stuart Mill and Harriet Taylor – but a brief and highly selective account of the private lives of some of the pioneers must be given in order to see what moral (if any) emerges from their morals, as one might say.

The honour of producing the first English journal supporting women's emancipation belongs to Richard Carlile and his 'moral wife', Eliza (Isis) Sharples. Richard Carlile (1790–1843) is best known for his championship of freedom of the press. The amazing thing is, considering the temper of the times, that he won his private war against authority, though at the cost of spending years in prison. In 1817, the year of the suspension of habeas corpus and the passing of the 'Gagging' Acts, Carlile took over a Fleet Street shop which sold Cobbett's *Political Register*, the latter having fled to America. Carlile not only proceeded to sell the *Political Register*, which Cobbett continued to edit from the U.S.A. for two further years, but also sold copies of the radical *Black Dwarf*, which was more to his liking than the *Register*, and when Steill, publisher of the *Black Dwarf*, was arrested, Carlile offered to take his place. In addition, he published some of William Hone's parodies of the Lord's Prayer and other sacred writings. He was kept in prison for eighteen weeks while Hone was prosecuted for blasphemous libel, and was eventually released on Hone's acquittal. In the meantime, his legal wife, Jane, had kept open the Fleet Street shop.

On his release, Carlile commenced publishing Tom Paine's *Rights of Man, Age of Reason* and other works. His real sin was to publish cheaply. Paine's works were included in the *Register* and also sold separately in cheap parts. The attitude of the authorities was that publications at a price which could be afforded by educated gentlemen only could do no harm but that radical or deistic writings which were likely to reach the common people were subversive. This attitude persists today with, perhaps, the substitution of the young and impressionable for the 'common people'. In November 1967, the publishers of *Last Exit to Brooklyn* were found guilty under the Obscene Publications Act, 1959, after trial at the Central Criminal Court. (This verdict was subsequently reversed on appeal.) According to the report of Judge Graham Rogers's summing up in *The Times* of 23.11.1967, the following transpired:

> Referring to the price of the novel, the Judge said this was important. The jury would pay regard to the words in the Act 'Persons who are likely, having regard to all the relevant circumstances, to read it'. This was not a shilling or half-crown novel, but a hardback selling at £1.10.0. a copy.

In 1819 Carlile was indicted for blasphemy and commenced a long struggle for freedom of the press against both the establishment and the Society for the Suppression of Vice (commonly called 'the Vice Society'), which had been founded by William Wilberforce in 1802. In August 1819, he took over the *Register* completely from its former publisher, Sherwin, becoming both publisher and editor and changing its name to the *Republican;* he also started issuing the

Deist. In spite of repeated fines and imprisonment, Carlile, aided by his wife and other volunteers, continued to sell radical and deist literature. The Fleet Street shop was the centre of the struggle until 1825 and shopman after shopman was arrested for selling banned publications. At one time, the shopmen operated from behind a screen to avoid identification by members of the 'Vice Society', who would make purchases in order to lay information. Between 1820 and 1823 the opposition included a Constitutional Association, supported by the Duke of Wellington, which was formed to suppress seditious publications, but a group of radical lawyers took up the cause of the defendants and made prosecution too expensive a pastime for the Tories of the Constitutional Association. So many shopmen were arrested and imprisoned in Newgate Jail that in September 1824 they began to edit the *Newgate Monthly Magazine*, which was published at Carlile's shop. At the end of 1824, the Government gave up and in November 1825 Carlile was released from prison unconditionally, in spite of not having paid his fines and refusing to enter into any recognizances regarding his future behaviour. From that time onwards the *Age of Reason* and many other previously banned works were allowed to circulate without hindrance.

As well as supporting freedom of the press by publishing radical and blasphemous literature, Carlile advocated the abolition of the monarchy, secular education, birth control and, as has been indicated, the emancipation of women. In 1829 he joined forces with the Reverend Robert Taylor, an Anglican priest who had become a deist. On return from an 'infidel tour' of industrial districts, the two men leased the Rotunda in Blackfriars Road for radical and free-thought activities. Again in gaol in 1831, Carlile was approached by a convert he had made during his 'infidel tour', a Miss Eliza Sharples, who reopened the Rotunda for him and gave lectures there on free-thought and women's emancipation under the name of 'Isis'. She also produced a journal, the *Isis*, which succeeded Carlile's current journal, the *Prompter*. Carlile and 'Isis' Sharples were obviously greatly attracted to one another and it appears that the former had broken with his wife, Jane, in 1830, a year before Eliza Sharples came to London. In 1832 Carlile was able to make provision for Jane through a legacy which he made over to her and he and Eliza agreed to live together on his release from prison, so 'Isis' Sharples became Richard Carlile's 'moral wife'. There were children of both unions and Carlile seems to have been an affectionate parent. He does not appear to have agonized over the irregularity of his second union in the way some of his contemporaries did in similar circumstances, perhaps partly on account of his temperament and partly on account of his working-class background, 'common law' marriages not being uncommon amongst working people nor excessively deplored.

Carlile's feminism was part of a syndrome of advanced or extreme ideas, which were insufficiently precise and co-ordinated to meet the approval of the intellectual radicals of his day. Like many another atheist and freethinker, he developed his own brand of religion at the end of his life and ended by calling himself the Reverend Richard Carlile. The publication in 1826 (possibly preceded by an earlier edition) of *Every Woman's Book*, giving contraceptive advice, puts him amongst the early birth controllers. His union with 'Isis' Sharples was due to no profounder cause than the collapse of his marriage and their mutual attraction, but once again the pattern of feminism and irregular morals was repeated.

Just as feminist ideas were inherent in radical thought, with its support of individual rights, so were they inherent in socialism, with its ideals of equality and support of the downtrodden. Robert Owen (1771–1858) advocated equality for women and an easing of the marriage laws. He lived to see the institution of Divorce Courts but was considerably in advance of the law, as he believed that what we should now call 'incompatibility of temperament' or 'breakdown of marriage' should be grounds for divorce. Like some moderns, he was in favour of making marriage more difficult and divorce easier. In *The New Moral World* (1838) he proposed that marriage should not be entered into without three months' public notice. No separation would be permissible within the first year of marriage, after which six months' notice had to be given, making a minimum period of eighteen months. Owen felt that there was no reason why persons should live together when at enmity and that after legal separation, remarriage should be possible. The communal care of children over three years of age, which he envisaged in his schemes for co-operative or communal living, eliminated one of the major objections to divorce.

Owen's thought on the subject of relations between the sexes was not entirely consistent. On occasion, he would speak as if he accepted the Platonic doctrine of wives in common, but in *The New Moral World* he made it clear that marriage should be formal. His views were undoubtedly feminist and 'advanced' but, naturally, he was not free from all the prejudices of his time and it comes as a shock to find that his 'New Harmony' was open to all the world except 'persons of colour'.

Perhaps one should include George Eliot (1819–1880) amongst the feminists with irregular morals, but the novelist was a somewhat lukewarm supporter of the women's cause, in spite of her friendship with those noted feminists, Bessie Rayner Parkes and Barbara Bodichon. Also, her liaison with George Henry Lewes became so profoundly respectable that even Queen Victoria was constrained to acknowledge it. Her friendship with Barbara Bodichon proved to be a lifelong one and Madame Bodichon is said to be the model of her *Romola*.

Marian Evans (to give George Eliot her real name) believed in fair play for women but considered that they needed to educate and improve themselves before they were fit to accept responsibility. Essentially puritanical, she yet had the moral courage to live with George Lewes as his wife. She was not of the stuff of which Bohemians are made and was no advertisement for the gay life; indeed, she was scarcely equipped for it, being serious and somewhat plain. Some friendships (including that of Harriet Martineau) were lost through her association with Lewes but her talent was such that public interest centred mainly on that, rather than on her private life, which was somewhat belatedly rehabilitated by her marriage to John Cross. Her energies went into her work as a novelist but in spite of her feminism being muted, no outstanding woman of her period could avoid affecting current thought on the position of women.

It was not just the virtual indissolubility of marriage which exercised the early feminists but also the complete legal control of a husband over his wife and children, both as to property and person. An over-simplification of the position would be to say that in return for his duty to maintain his wife, a husband had the right to custody of her person, to consortium and service, the right to chastise her within certain limits and to take over her property and earnings, if any. It was, however, possible for a wealthy father, through the use of trusts, to prevent a son-in-law running through capital settled on his daughter. Average nineteenth-century practice was, of course, considerably in advance of the requirements of the law, but as late as 1840 the courts upheld a Mr Cochrane who had imprisoned his wife. Mrs Cochrane had previously left her husband but had been tricked into visiting him and was then prevented from leaving. Mr Justice Coleridge maintained that the husband's rights included 'enforcing co-habitation and a common residence'. (*Re* Cochrane, (1840) 8 Dowl. 630, 636.)

A modicum of relief came with the Matrimonial Causes Act of 1857, which extended to the well-to-do middle-class the privilege of divorce which the wealthy aristocrats had formerly obtained by Act of Parliament, at the same time allowing maintenance to an injured wife. For substantial advance in the direction of freedom of person wives had to wait until the latter part of the century. In 1878 Parliament, disturbed by the continuing brutality of the 'Kicking District' of Liverpool, with its annual toll of working-class women kicked to death by their husbands, passed a further Matrimonial Causes Act allowing a legal separation, with maintenance, to wives whose husbands had been convicted of aggravated assault. The middle-class woman's relief came with the Jackson case of 1891 (Regina *v* Jackson, *Ex parte* Jackson (1891) 1 Q.B. 671, 679). Mrs Jackson had left her husband and had refused to obey an order for the restitution of conjugal rights. Mr Jackson managed to capture and imprison her but her relatives issued a writ of habeas corpus against him. Current opinion believed that Jackson had acted within his legal rights but the Court of Appeal reversed the Cochrane judgment, not only holding that no British subject had the right to imprison another, whether his wife or not, but also that 'such quaint and absurd dicta as are to be found in the books as to the right of a husband over his wife in respect of personal chastisement are not, I think, now capable of being cited as authorities in the Courts of Justice in this or any other civilized country'.

The fulminations of the feminists against the marriage laws do not make sense unless seen in the context of the personal situation of wives before 1891 and it was, of course, in cases where marriages were unhappy that the marriage laws became important.

Various unhappy wives managed to escape, despite the rigours of the law; perhaps, on occasion, their husbands were glad to be rid of them. One that got away was Anna Wheeler, who was to inspire William Thompson to write the most important feminist publication between Mary Wollstonecraft's *Vindication* of 1792 and John Stuart Mill's *Subjection of Women* of 1869, namely, his *Appeal of One Half of the Human Race, Women, against the Pretensions of the Other Half, Men, to Restrain them in Political and thence in Civil and Domestic Slavery* (1825).

Both Anna Wheeler and William Thompson derived from the Irish Protestant ascendancy. Anna Doyle, as the former then was, married, at the age of fifteen, a youth of nineteen, Francis Massy Wheeler, who soon showed himself to be a hopeless alcoholic. The joint household lasted for twelve years, during which period Anna bore six children, two only (both girls) surviving. The home was not a happy one. It was shared by Anna's sister, Bessie, and the two women appear to have quarrelled over the children. Anna Wheeler managed to keep abreast of contemporary thought, having books sent to her from London. Contemporary Irish society commiserated with her husband for having a studious wife; she ought to have absorbed herself wholly in the activities of her husband, who divided his time between his stables and drinking, letting his property go to rack and ruin. The home was broken up by Anna, her sister and daughters joining her uncle, the Governor of Guernsey. Once away from Ireland, Anna's personality flowered and she was a brilliant success in the cosmopolitan society of Guernsey Government House. She left Guernsey in 1816, staying first in France and later in London and became a prominent figure in Saint-Simonian circles on both sides of the Channel, forming a link between the French socialists and the Owenites in England.

In 1832 the Saint-Simonians sent 'missionaries' to England and both these and the Owenites suffered virulent attacks on account of their alleged immorality. A critic of socialism, Edward Hancock, accused both groups of wishing to instruct females in the art of prostitution and of ignoring the fact that if fathers did not know the identity of their daughters, incestuous relations could result.[1] The situation was not so horrific as this but the Saint-Simonians in England proclaimed the need for reform of the marriage laws and for the provision of divorce. Mrs Wheeler translated an article on the emancipation of women from the French women's periodical, *La Femme Libre*, for Robert Owen's co-operative journal, *Crisis*.

That somewhat neglected socialist, William Thompson, claimed to have been inspired by Anna Wheeler in the same way as John Stuart Mill was later to attribute much of his best thought to Harriet Taylor. He dedicated his *Appeal* to Mrs Wheeler, attributing the greater part of its contents to 'her mind', the remainder being 'joint property'. The *Appeal* was a refutation of James Mill's contention that the interests of women could be included in those of their fathers or husbands. In an introductory letter to Mrs Wheeler, published with the *Appeal*, Thompson wrote:

> Weary of waiting, the protest of at least one man and one woman is here put forward against doctrines which disgrace the principle of utility; the facts are denied and the inferences controverted even if the facts are true. Could any thing bring the principal of utility, or the search of the greatest amount of preponderant good, into disrepute, it would be the peculiarly inconsistent conduct of its abettors. . . .[2]

and later:

> But I hear you indignantly reject the boon of equality with such creatures as men now are. With you I would equally elevate both sexes.[3]

Both Thompson and Anna Wheeler tended to attribute the degraded position of women to the economic system and to feel that a socialist society was necessary for women to attain equality with men. Their thought was much more daring than that of the main body of feminists, which organized the women's movement in England during the second half of the nineteenth century.

Mrs Wheeler was fortunate in having a position in society and in attracting admiration, as well as criticism. She was a great beauty but her daughter Rosina (Lady Lytton) wrote of her, 'I don't think she much valued her beauty'.[4] Disraeli is said to have described her as 'something between Jeremy Bentham and Meg Merrilies, very clever, but awfully revolutionary'. It was the 'awfully revolutionary' element in Anna Wheeler's make-up which gave rise to criticism of the same sort as was levelled at Mary Wollstonecraft and

Jacobins generally. Her daughter Rosina speaks of her as 'unfortunately deeply imbued with the pernicious fallacies of the French Revolution, which had then more or less seared their trace through Europe, and who was besides strongly tainted by the corresponding poison of Mrs Wollstonecraft's book'.[5] Surprisingly, a relatively modern writer, Michael Sadleir,[6] seems to accept this assessment and portrays Anna Wheeler as a monster of selfishness, attributing much of Rosina Lytton's unhappy fate to her mother's influence. Quite obviously, in the domestic setting, Anna Wheeler was a square peg in a round hole. Her metier was amongst advanced socialist thinkers; the French crowned her as 'The Goddess of Reason'. Her habit of referring to Christ as 'our Eastern philosopher' could scarcely endear her to conventional society. Information concerning her life is less full than one could wish. William Thompson manifestly admired and adored her. She had her successes to balance her misfortunes and does not seem to have suffered in the way which Mary Wollstonecraft did, although her views were far more outrageous. Perhaps this is because personal scandal did not touch her in the same way, or perhaps her twelve years of matrimony were such that the rest of her life seemed agreeable in comparison. William Thompson holds an honoured place in the history of British socialism and is being increasingly appreciated.

The rights of fathers over their children were complete at the beginning of the nineteenth century and were the occasion of bringing Caroline Norton (1808–1877) into the history of feminism. Though she might well have denied it, one can scarcely believe that Caroline would have campaigned for the rights of mothers and provoked an Infants' Custody Act had it not been for her unhappy marriage to George Norton. Born a Sheridan and without a dowry, she was glad enough, at the age of nineteen, to make what seemed a reasonable match with George Norton, who had been in love with her for some time. The couple were peculiarly illsuited, as it turned out. The beautiful, witty, reckless, tactless and tempestuous Caroline, with her Whig connections, found herself unable to respect her cautious, mean, obstinate Tory husband who, she found, was subject to outbursts of rage which could lead to physical violence. There were faults on both sides but it is difficult to excuse George Norton for taking away their three children from Caroline and depriving her of access to them, in order to impose on his wife a financial settlement advantageous to himself. Caroline's fight with her pen for custody of her children and Sergeant Talfourd's campaign in Parliament are well known. Not only did the Infants' Custody Act of 1839 owe much to her but the 1857 Act reforming the marriage and divorce laws was influenced in the direction of protecting the earnings and position of deserted, separated or divorced wives through two pamphlets she brought out in 1854 and 1855 respectively.

Two outstanding scandals were associated with Mrs Norton. When George Norton brought suit against Lord Melbourne for alienation of his wife's affections, shock waves reverberated throughout the chancelleries of Europe. It was not every day that a British prime minister was involved in such an action. The suit was dismissed but Caroline's reputation was not untarnished. Lacking a legal personality as a married woman, her interests could not be represented at court. It is still uncertain whether Norton's motives in sueing Melbourne were personal or political. The other scandal, primarily a political one, related to Caroline's friendship with Sidney Herbert and the unfounded rumour that she had given secret information to *The Times* in December 1845, regarding the Cabinet's decision to repeal the Corn Laws. This allegation was later revived through George Meredith's *Diana of the Crossways*, said to be based on Caroline's life.

It must have been irritating for a genuine feminist, such as Harriet Martineau, to find that a society woman like Caroline Norton, who did not believe in the equality of the sexes, had made the outstanding contribution of the period towards women's rights. Also, Caroline's literary reputation was far from negligible, even if it did not quite equal that of Miss Martineau. No charge of immorality was ever proved against Caroline but she was a target of criticism most of her life as the result of her matrimonial difficulties. She did not take things lying down, and as *Punch* (30.6.1877) wrote after her death:

> And hate and envy gave their tongues free play
>   On the proud soul that would not be O'er-borne
> But strove to show brave face to bleakest day,
>   And hid her wounds, and gave back scorn for scorn.

Essentially a 'man's woman', remarrying at the age of sixty-nine, two years after George Norton's death, Caroline Norton (like Anna Wheeler) was in some ways more in the French than the English style. One might think that her life provided ample ammunition for those who wished to associate feminism with easy virtue but as well as not believing in sex equality, Caroline was no radical and the abuse she received was personal, coming mainly from those who upheld her husband's cause.

Notes

1 Hancock, Edward, *Robert Owen's Community System, Etc., and the Horrid Doings of the St Simonians*, 1832, 35; and Pankhurst, Richard K.P., 'Saint-Simonism in England', in *The Twentieth Century*, Dec. 1952 and Jan. 1953.

2 Thompson, William, *Appeal of One Half of the Human Race, Women, against the Pretensions of the Other Half, Men, to Restrain them in Political and thence in Civil and Domestic Slavery*, 1825, ix *et seq.*

3 *Ibid.*

4 Devey, Louisa, *Life of Rosina, Lady Lytton*, 1887, 3.

5 *Ibid.*, 8.

6 Sadleir, Michael, *Bulwer Lytton and His Wife*, 1933.

5

The South Place Congregation

God be thanked, the meanest of his creatures,
Boasts two soul-sides, one to face the world with,
One to show a woman when he loves her.

Robert Browning

Many of the early feminists were to be found amongst a group of
Unitarians, living in London but largely drawn from families
originating in East Anglia. These included Harriet Martineau and a
circle revolving around the preacher, William Johnson Fox, which
included Harriet Taylor (née Hardy, later to become Mrs John
Stuart Mill) and the highly gifted (but, alas, consumptive) Flower
sisters, Sarah and Eliza. One might have thought that such a group
would have provided an example of almost puritanical rectitude (as,
of course, Harriet Martineau and many of Fox's congregation did),
but Fox himself, Eliza Flower and Harriet Taylor all managed to
involve themselves in complications, the complications being
mutual in the first two instances.

The Unitarian journal was the *Monthly Repository*, to which
Fox's associates contributed and which he took over in 1831 with a
view to developing it into a periodical of a general, rather than
parochial, interest. The gifted circle included Robert Browning, who
was drawn into it through love for Lizzie Flower, nine years his
senior. In 1829 Fox became guardian of the Flower girls on the
death of their father and also fell in love with Lizzie, who returned
his affection. Fox was unhappily married, and presumably as a
result of his experience, became an advocate of divorce.

Harriet Taylor, who was a close friend of Lizzie Flower, became
increasingly dissatisfied with her estimable but prosaic husband and

sought advice from Fox who, instead of trying to reconcile her to her situation, as one would think any pastor would feel to be his duty, decided to introduce her to John Stuart Mill, the result of which is well known. Her feminist views, subsequently to have such an important influence on John Mill, seem to have developed during this period and she also came to question the marriage laws, possibly partly on account of her friend Lizzie Flower's difficulties and partly because of her own situation. She wrote in 1832 or thereabouts:

> In the present system of habits and opinions girls enter into what is called a contract perfectly ignorant of the conditions of it, and that they should be so is considered absolutely essential to their fitness for it.[1]

Also, possibly in the draft of a letter to John Mill:

> Women are educated for one single object, to gain their living by marrying (some poor souls get it without church going in the same way – they do not seem to me a bit worse than their honoured sisters) – to be married is the object of their existence and that being gained they do really cease to exist as to anything worth calling life or any useful purpose.[2]

Interest lies in the conflicting ways in which the two couples dealt with their moral problems.

Mrs Fox, who had retreated to the upper portion of the house which contained her husband, children and her husband's wards, the Flower girls, at last rebelled and, in 1832, demanded a separation, only to be told that finance would not permit of separate establishments. In 1834 on the marriage of Sallie Flower (remembered today as the composer of the hymn, 'Nearer, my God, to Thee') she could no longer tolerate the situation and complained to her husband's congregation. Fox resigned, though disputing his congregation's right to concern itself in his domestic affairs. An investigation was made, after which Fox was invited to withdraw his resignation and did so. A sizeable minority quit the Church on account of his conduct and views, for he was on record in the *Monthly Repository* as favouring the conversion of marriage into a civil contract, which could be ended if the marriage were to break down. In 1833, in 'The Dissenting Marriage Question', he wrote:

> If they [Dissenters] can induce the legislature to adopt the theory that the marriage contract is a common, in distinction from a

religious, engagement, [it] should be regarded by the law merely as
a civil ceremony. . . . A civil contract, not dissoluble when its dissolution is required by the interests of the contracting parties and
of the community would be a strange anomaly.[3]

Fox contended that there was a Biblical sanction for divorce and
seems to have believed that the indissolubility of marriage was a
cause of prostitution: 'Even a temporary toleration of polygamy
would be better, infinitely better, than this eternal flood of prostitution.'[4]

One might have thought that the successful weathering of the
storm at South Place Chapel would have induced caution, but in
1835 Fox became formally separated from his wife and moved to a
house in Bayswater with Eliza Flower and two of his children. This
resulted in his expulsion from the Association of Presbyterian
Ministers in London, the members of which were mainly Unitarian.
He continued to be the preacher at South Place Chapel until 1852
but ceased describing himself as 'the Reverend'. The change in his
affairs proved to be a liberation and Fox continued with his journal-
ism and lectured widely. In 1847, the year following the death of
Eliza Flower, he entered Parliament as the Radical member for
Oldham.

We are given to understand that the relationship between
William Fox and Eliza Flower was 'innocent', though this is rather
hard to swallow in view of their setting up house together. Apparently there were suggestions of misconduct in 1834 when Mrs
Fox's complaint was considered by the South Place congregation.
John Stuart Mill thought the allegations should be denied but Fox
was much less cautious than Mill and the form of his denial was
hardly helpful. Crabb Robinson, a Unitarian, wrote:

> I have been reading the printed papers in Fox's affair with his wife
> in which he appears to have pushed frankness and sincerity to an
> extremity – He did not scruple to avow that though no illicit inter-
> course had in fact taken place between him and his friend (Miss
> Flower) it was merely accidental, there being nothing in their
> principles against so acting – only prudence was against.[5]

The case for the 'innocence' of the Fox/Flower relationship rests on
the transparent honesty of the participants and some letters of the

Flower sisters. Richard Garnett writes concerning the move to Bayswater:

> The step unquestionably involved no blemish of personal purity. No reader of the letters of Eliza and her sister can have any doubt on this point: nor would a person of the independence and intrepidity of Eliza Flower have submitted to an ambiguous relation. She would have assumed his name and declared herself his wife in the sight of Heaven.[6]

Feminist views were part of Fox's radicalism and were not limited to his dislike of the marriage laws. In the *Monthly Repository* of September 1832 he published an article, 'A Political and Social Anomaly', castigating the lack of logic in a situation where women were without votes but a woman was destined to inherit the throne in the near future:

> Is it not strange that the egregious anomaly should have been felt of institutions which sometimes invest woman, educated in very unfavourable circumstances, with the state and amplitude of supreme political authority; and which, nevertheless, uniformly deny to woman, though trained in the most favourable circumstances, the exercise of the very lowest and simplest political function, that which is essential to political existence, the elective franchise. In the common opinion of common statesmen, the fitness of women to vote for an individual's elevation to the temporary dignity of a legislator in the House of Commons, is a mere joke: yet her naming of scores of persons legislators for life, and all their heirs legislators too, through all generations, is an essential portion of that perfection of ancestral wisdom under which we live. She is vested with the entire power of the State, or not entrusted with its meanest fraction.[7]

In the course of this highly feminist article, Fox echoed the sentiments of Mary Wollstonecraft and heralded those of John Stuart Mill:

> In his [man's] disgust at female pretension, (not a jot worse than male pretension; and either, only disgusting because unfounded), he has crippled female intellect, and thereby enfeebled his own. In training a dependant, he has lost a companion. In the passing admiration of superficial accomplishment, he has foregone the permanent advantage of solid attainment.[8]

Again, in the following year, he wrote even more decisively:

> ... and man, three-quarters civilised, which is as far as we are got, educates her [woman] for pleasure and dependency, keeps her in a state of pupilage, closes against her most of the avenues of self-support, and cheats her by the false forms of an irrevocable contract into a life of subserviance to his will. The reason for all which is 'that he is the stronger'.[9]

In contrast, John Stuart Mill and Harriet reached a somewhat uneasy accommodation with the aggrieved husband, John Taylor. Harriet tried for a time, in 1832, to take her husband's advice and give up Mill, but concluded or convinced herself that the separation was ruining Mill's talent, so gave up the attempt and her admirer was readmitted to the Taylor establishment. Harriet would neither give up her husband and children nor give up Mill; her husband did not force the issue. After a period when the shared companionship provided by Mill's frequent visits to the Taylor household proved somewhat unsatisfactory, John Taylor provided his wife with a house near Bromley where she could stay (accompanied by her daughter Helen) and entertain Mill, returning to the Taylor household for her sons' school holidays and other family occasions. From that time onwards until John Taylor's death Harriet had either two husbands or none at all, depending on how one looks at it. There is some written evidence pointing to a Platonic relationship between Harriet and Mill and also something in Mill's character which makes this seem credible.[10]

Contemporary Victorian opinion speculated on whether an illicit relationship existed between the couple or whether Mill lacked sexual drive, eventually veering towards the latter presumption. Probably the course taken, especially as Mill was eventually able to marry Harriet after John Taylor's death, did less harm to his contemporary reputation and work than an outright liaison would have done. As it was, Mill's sensitive reaction to criticism led to his temporary withdrawal from society.

Both Mill and Harriet looked upon sexual relations as a personal matter which should be considered unimportant to all but those immediately concerned and shared a measure of disgust at the way in which women were more or less set aside for marriage and usually given little say in how this should be arranged. Also, they were affected by Malthusian thought and believed that population problems resulted from lack of self-control, increased prosperity resulting in increased breeding. Mill's repudiation, on his engagement, of the legal rights which he would obtain through marriage, is well known but is nonetheless worth quoting.

> Being about, if I am so happy as to obtain her consent, to enter into the marriage relation with the only woman I have ever known, with whom I would have entered into that state; and the whole character of the marriage relation as constituted by law being such as both she and I entirely and conscientiously disapprove, for this amongst other reasons, that it confers upon one of the parties to the contract, legal power over the person, property and freedom of action of the other party, independent of her own wishes and will; I legally having no means of divesting myself of these odious powers (as I most assuredly would do if an engagement to this effect could be made legally binding by me) feel it my duty to put on record a formal protest against the existing law of marriage, in so far as conferring such powers; and a solemn promise never in any case or under any circumstances to use them. And in the event of marriage between Mrs. Taylor and me I declare it to be my will and intention, and the condition of the engagement between us, that she retains in all respects whatever the same absolute freedom of action, and freedom of disposal of herself and of all that does or may at any time belong to her, as if no such marriage had taken place; and I absolutely disclaim and repudiate all pretension to have acquired any *rights* whatever by virtue of such marriage.[11]

While Mill and Harriet both believed they ought to be able to rise superior to the lusts of the flesh and no doubt felt they were making a great renunciation in doing so during John Taylor's lifetime, there was no reason for the conventionally minded John Taylor, who had been a good and generous husband, to like any of this and one can only wonder at the magnanimous way in which he dealt with what was, from his point of view, a thoroughly unsatisfactory situation. Perhaps he had had enough of high thinking and overcharged emotions when he arranged for his wife to go to a separate house in Bromley and hankered after a more placid way of life.

Harriet, also, owing to her husband's generosity, lost less than she would have done if she had left her husband and lived with Mill as his wife – but who can estimate the cost of the loss of intimacy during (to use a banal phrase) the best years of their lives? Harriet was not cut off from her children and although criticized, probably had much less to put up with than would have been the case had she lived with Mill. Divorce was not a practical possibility, Divorce Courts not being set up until 1857. If the arrangement seems odd to us, it seemed odd to contemporary society also. The educational gap between the average man and woman was so great at the time that the sort of intellectual friendship and working collaboration which existed between John Mill and Harriet Taylor and which ran parallel with their affection was well-nigh incomprehensible.

While Mill may have been ardent when young, his temperament and conduct were so far removed from licentiousness that it was impossible for his association with feminism to be taken as an illustration of an affinity between the feminist idea and loose morals. The tendency, in hostile quarters, was to look upon Mill as a desiccated intellectual, capable of more sexual self-control than the average man, and also a bit of a crank. The average, robust man, it was felt, would not share his unnecessarily sensitive concern for women and his championship of their cause was considered part and parcel of his crankiness.

The importance to feminism of the Mill/Taylor affair lies in Harriet's conversion of Mill from an abstract to a practical supporter of women's emancipation. Mill puts it like this in his *Autobiography:*

> It might be supposed . . . that my strong convictions on the complete equality in all legal, political, social and domestic relations, which ought to exist between men and women, may have been adopted or learnt from her [Harriet]. This was so far from being the fact, that those convictions were among the earliest results of the application of my mind to political subjects, and the strength with which I held them was, I believe, more than anything else, the originating cause of the interest she felt in me. What is true is that, until I knew her, the opinion was in my mind little more than an abstract principle . . . that perception of the vast practical bearings of women's disabilities which found expression in the book on *The Subjection of Women* was acquired mainly through her teaching.[12]

The feminist idea was implicit in Utilitarianism, as Jeremy Bentham appreciated, for the greatest happiness of the greatest number could scarcely exclude half the human race unless it were argued (as, indeed, has been the case at times) that women were less than human. As Mill admits, he had not taken the matter seriously until he came under the influence of Harriet, who, in her turn, had been readily influenced by the ideas circulating among the élite of William Johnson Fox's South Place congregation. Mill's home background was scarcely such that he would be directed towards feminism, for his father, James Mill, treated his unintellectual wife with contempt and made a much-publicized contribution to the *Encyclopaedia Britannica* (Supplement to the 4th (1824) edition) in which he stated, when discussing groups not in need of parliamentary representation, 'In this light also women may be regarded, the interests of almost all of whom are involved in that of their fathers or that of their husbands.' (This is the 'celebrated article on Government' to which William Thompson took exception.)

In view of the paucity of writings emanating from Mrs John Stuart Mill, there has been considerable speculation concerning the extent of her inspiration and influence. Such writings as there are, however, around the year 1828 (although nothing was published until 1831) contain the feminist ideas later put forward by Mill in his *Subjection of Women* (1869), which derived, in essence, from Harriet's 'The Enfranchisement of Women' (*Westminster Review*, 1851). It appears that Harriet made the deliberate decision, on resuming her association with Mill after the break in 1832, to devote her abilities to the furtherance of Mill's greater genius, rather than to follow her own literary aspirations. Recent research tends to confirm Mill's own assessment of his wife's influence on all his work, apart from his *Logic*, and as Michael St John Packe says: 'It is difficult on the face of it to see why Mill, who was so soberly and carefully exact in every other matter, should be discredited in this.'[13]

It is quite possible that Mill might eventually have become an active supporter of women's emancipation even if he had not met Harriet but it seems unlikely he would have felt so strongly about it. Mill was in love with another man's wife at a time when divorce was a matter for the Church and an Act of Parliament was necessary to enable divorced persons to remarry. Mill and Harriet perceived that the difficulty went further than the state of the law and was inherent in the economic and social order; it was hopeless to suggest that inclination, not law, should bind man and wife together while wives and children were economically dependent upon the husband and father. Mill wrote:

> The first and indispensable step, therefore, towards the enfranchisement of woman, is that she be so educated, as not to be dependent either on her father or husband for subsistence. It does not follow that a woman should *actually* support herself because she should be *capable* of doing so.[14]

John Stuart Mill's career extended into the main period of the women's emancipation movement; he was to present the women's first petition for the vote in 1866 and to move the amendment of the 1867 Reform Bill in favour of women; also, he volunteered to give evidence before the Royal Commission on the Contagious Diseases Acts, which reported in 1870, and spoke in support of Josephine Butler and the other abolitionists (see Chapter 9); his *Subjection of Women* was to become the feminists' textbook. He had a tendency to temper his support of unpopular causes with discretion. This applied, in particular, to birth control, after an early, unfortunate experience. He was not a man like Frederick Pethick Lawrence of the suffragette era, prepared to suffer imprisonment, the horrors of hunger-striking and financial loss for the women's cause, but he gave substantial help and his intellectual pre-eminence causes him to be looked upon as the most important male advocate of women's emancipation.

It will be seen that in this period of early feminism, many of the great debates of Victorian moral and intellectual life were anticipated. Freedom of the press, freethought and atheism, birth control, radicalism and socialism, were all linked, sometimes by the personal circumstances of those involved, with that questioning of the marriage laws and the position of women which continued throughout the century.

Notes

1 Hayek, F. A., *John Stuart Mill and Harriet Taylor: Their Correspondence and Subsequent Marriage*, 1951, 77.

2 *Ibid.*, 76–7.

3 Fox, William Johnson, 'The Dissenting Marriage Question', in *Monthly Repository*, 1833, 139 and 141.

4 *Ibid.*, 142.

5 Mineka, F. E., *The Dissidence of Dissent*, 1944, 194.

6 Garnett, Richard, *The Life of W. J. Fox*, 1910, 166.

7 Fox, William Johnson, 'A Political and Social Anomaly', in *Monthly Repository*, 1832, 638.

8 *Ibid.*, 641.

9 *Ibid.*, 1833, 177.

10 St John Packe, Michael, *The Life of John Stuart Mill*, 1954, 125.

11 Hayek, *op. cit.*, 168.

12 Mill, John Stuart, *Autobiography*, 1908, 140.

13 St John Packe, *op. cit.*, 316.

14 Hayek, *op. cit.*, 65.

1 Harriet Taylor *c*1844 *Miniature in British Library of Political and Economic Science*

2 John Stuart Mill *c*1858 *Radio Times Hulton Picture Library*

6

Divorce and the Double Moral Standard

What is sauce for the goose is sauce for the gander.

Proverb

By the time divorce was made accessible to the middle-classes, the main women's emancipation movement was under way, but the feminists cannot take credit for the extension of divorce possibilities. Indeed, the Matrimonial Causes Act of 1857, which set up the first civil Divorce Courts in England, was in many ways a setback to the feminists, as it frustrated their attempts to secure a Married Women's Property Act.

In 1855 the Law Amendment Society introduced a Married Women's Property Bill into the House of Commons which proposed to allow married women the same right to make wills and hold property as their unmarried sisters possessed. The Society had taken up the issue largely as the result of a pamphlet, drawn up and printed by Barbara Bodichon (formerly Barbara Leigh Smith), called *A Brief Summary in Plain Language of the Most Important Laws Concerning Women* (1855). A women's committee was formed by Mme Bodichon to collect signatures and organize a petition in support of the measure. The main period of the women's emancipation movement may be said to date from the formation of this committee in 1855, although there had already been activity in the fields of education, emigration and employment.

The Married Women's Property Bill did not succeed in passing its second reading until 1857, but in that year a Matrimonial Causes Bill was sponsored by the Government and became law, containing (in addition to the main provisions for divorce) the possibility of certain property rights being granted to separated or divorced wives. It was then held that the injustice to married women, who had been neglected or deserted by their husbands, had been relieved and that a Married Women's Property Act was no longer necessary. No Property Act was passed until 1870, when a beginning was made by allowing married women to retain personal earnings in employment carried on separately from their husbands or obtained by the exercise of literary, artistic or scientific skill.

Although the Matrimonial Causes Act of 1857 owed little to feminist agitation, apart from Caroline Norton's successful campaign for protecting the position and earnings of deserted, separated and divorced wives, it was important to the feminist movement because it put the double moral standard in the definitive form of statute law. In so doing, it gave the feminists something to 'bite on', in the same way as the 1832 Reform Bill, by including the enfranchisement of 'male persons' for the first time in statute law, provided a focal point for the opposition by the advocates of women's suffrage. Just as the Reform Bill enacted the custom that men should vote and women should not, so the Matrimonial Causes Act enshrined the precedents followed by the House of Lords in considering Bills of Divorcement, to the effect that adultery alone was a reason for a man divorcing his wife but that adultery needed to be supplemented by some other offence, such as cruelty or desertion, for a woman to have grounds to divorce her husband. The justification for the double standard was given by the Lord Chancellor, Lord Cranworth, in the following words:

> A wife might, without any loss of caste, and possibly with reference to the interests of her children, or even of her husband, condone an act of adultery on the part of the husband; but a husband could not condone a similar act on the part of a wife. No one would venture to suggest that a husband could possibly do so, and for this, among other reasons . . . that the adultery of the wife might be the means of palming spurious offspring upon the husband, while the adultery of the husband could have no such effect with regard to the wife.[1]

This type of justification for a double standard was often amplified by the statement that the husband's adultery did not affect the property and income of the family, whereas that of the wife, if resulting in 'spurious offspring', would do so.

The social implications of the attitude outlined by Lord Cranworth are interesting. If the adultery of the husband were to have no ill-effect upon family life, it must presumably be committed with a woman without family or who did not belong to the 'respectable classes' and whose family life was consequently considered to be unimportant. If the adultery were to occur with a woman of the same social class as the husband, he would risk planting 'spurious offspring' on a family which was presumably as socially valuable as his own. Obviously the remark was made in a context where upper- and middle-class men resorted, for their pleasures, to women of lower social station. The assumption that the property rights of the legitimate family were unaffected only held good if it were also assumed that the husband's adultery was with prostitutes or that he was conscienceless enough to make no provision for his mistress and illegitimate children, if any.

The danger to the family by the possible introduction of venereal disease through a husband's illicit affairs was normally ignored by those anxious to treat a husband's extra-marital adventures as unimportant, but this clearly could adversely affect the health and welfare of the whole family and even its income and property, through a diminution of the husband's earning power.

The double moral standard reflects the prime importance of property in a patriarchal society, at the expense of human values, and the ambivalent attitude of the law towards women. The zeal of the law in protecting the rights of legitimate offspring was matched by its cruelty towards the unmarried mother and her child. A husbandless woman, who could accomplish the difficult task of proving the paternity of her child to the satisfaction of the courts, was lucky if she could obtain half-a-crown a week from the father; one-and-sixpence was a more usual sum. The idiocy of a code of law which considered women so weak and irresponsible that they should not take part in public affairs and could not handle property but at the same time placed on the allegedly weaker sex the onus of resisting the advances of the stronger and the responsibility of bringing up illegitimate children practically unaided, seems wellnigh incredible. Progress in this area has been very slow. The

Harewood divorce case (1967) provoked speculation on whether the 'other woman' and illegitimate children should not be deemed to have rights as well as the legitimate family. The maximum that the father of an illegitimate child could be ordered by a Magistrates' Court to pay to the mother was limited to £2 10s a week, until the Maintenance Orders Act of 1968 removed the upper limit of such awards. It is still assumed that it is the duty of an unmarried mother to bring up her child on her own, apart from any maintenance award.

The feminist objection to the double moral standard tended, for a period, to become absorbed in the campaign against the Contagious Diseases Acts, and after the repeal of the Acts (see Chapter 9), the general campaign for Moral Welfare. It shows itself today in the opposition to such measures as the Street Offences Act of 1959 which regulates the prostitute but not her client nor males engaging in solicitation. In 1923 a Matrimonial Causes Act of that year removed the double standard from the divorce laws of England, bringing an equity between the sexes in this respect such as Scotland had enjoyed without apparent misadventure for over three hundred years. Socially, the double moral standard still lingers on, though the 'spurious offspring' argument lost its force once contraception came to be widely practised.

There were forces at work in Victorian times, both in this country and America, tending to build up the ideal of the purity of women. Men had traditionally allowed themselves a liberty of sexual experiment which they denied to the women of their own family, but the tendency in earlier times had been to harp upon the inherent wickedness of women and to consider they needed restraint for this to be kept in check. With a young Queen upon the English throne, to take this attitude seemed, to say the least, somewhat tactless, especially when Victoria was obviously a shining example of moral probity, compared with her Hanoverian predecessors. The standard changed and it became acceptable to look upon women, though weak and in need of protection, as pure and, like the Queen, the guardians of family life – the 'Angel in the House'. To some extent this could be held to justify the double moral standard. If women were naturally pure (apart from a certain degraded group) then the imposition of a high moral standard was no hardship or injustice. Also, if men were highly sexed but decent women were fundament-

ally incapable of enjoying sexual experience, then it was only reasonable that a greater freedom should be permitted to men than to
women. It was considered that a satisfactory relationship could be
the better attained if the woman came to marriage totally inexper-
ienced (could there be a fear of invidious comparisons?) and the
man had had some practice in sex relations; as initiative lay with the
man, the greater his experience, the better the marriage. Thus the
double moral standard was rationalized. If a woman showed an
active interest in sex, it was thought she had become depraved
through addiction to drink or some other cause.

The Victorian frame of mind had its influence both on the continent of Europe and the U.S.A., but in the latter country there were
other factors tending to build up the idea of the moral superiority of
women. The presence of the frontier with its heavy demands upon
American men, together with their dedication towards the building
up of industry, trade and commerce, led them to abrogate the
responsibility for cultural life and to hand over the job of civilizing
their communities to women. The result was that moral matters
were looked upon as largely the concern of women and they were
expected to have higher moral standards than men. As Myron
Brenton puts it:

> The oppressive nineteenth-century sexual double standard put the
> Victorian woman in a position of sexual inferiority – but, as we
> have seen, very much in a position of moral superiority.[2]

The feminist effort (of which more in subsequent chapters) was not
so much in the direction of easier divorce as towards pecuniary
justice for women on the dissolution of marriage and the raising of
the moral standards of men to those of respectable women. Millicent
Fawcett, the leader of the constitutional movement for women's
suffrage, was wont to point out that it was an insult to men for the
law to assume they were incapable of the moral standards expected
of women.

High and equal moral standards and justice for injured wives was
the object of the feminists from the 1850s onwards. So long as
marriage was a woman's meal ticket, pressure for easier divorce was
as likely to come from men, unhappy within the straitjacket of
Victorian marriage, as from women.

Notes

1 Parl. Deb. 1857, 3S, Vol. 145, c. 496 *et seq.*
2 Brenton, Myron, *The American Male*, 1967, 126.

7

The Mainstream

For while the tired waves, vainly breaking,
Seem here no painful inch to gain,
Far back, through creeks and inlets making,
Comes silent, flooding in, the main.

Arthur Hugh Clough

The period between 1855 and the outbreak of the First World War in 1914 saw a long and protracted struggle for women's rights. Progress was slow and piecemeal, so that the campaigners may well have felt, in moments of depression, that they 'seem no painful inch to gain'; the total effect, however, was that of a social revolution. This revolution in the position of women (though not effected entirely by the feminists) has had as much impact on the lives of ordinary people as the industrial revolution, which has been so much more frequently chronicled by the historians. Also, like the industrial revolution, it is an incomplete and continuing process.

The leaders of the women's emancipation movement during the second half of the nineteenth century, although they had some claim to be called 'advanced', did not deviate from the norm to the same extent as the early feminists. Indeed, in most instances their morals were impeccable and they could be looked upon as examples of Victorian rectitude. These women fought the battles for married women's property rights, education, entry to the professions and the vote with a considerable measure of success. At the beginning of the twentieth century the parliamentary vote still eluded them and some professions were still barred, but the local government vote had been won, women could become Poor Law Guardians and hold some other local offices, the 'siege of Cambridge' had broken the barriers to higher education, women could enter the medical profession and could work in many occupations from which they had previously been excluded.

It may be contended that the women's movement had more chance of success when its leaders were obviously respectable and worthy, rather than literary ladies with dubious morals, and it can scarcely be cause for criticism that the marriages of women such as Millicent Fawcett and Josephine Butler were happy. Nevertheless, there is a difference of opinion as to the effectiveness of the policy of trying to undermine one male bastion, then another, and a belief in some quarters that more far-reaching emancipation could have been attained had a concerted effort been made to re-structure society, including its moral basis, rather than to undertake piecemeal reform. This is not a matter that can be proved one way or another – one cannot experiment with history – but it is worthwhile examining the extent to which the feminists subscribed to conventional morality and the effect of this upon women's emancipation.

The tone of the women's movement was set, for much of the period, by women such as Millicent Garrett Fawcett, who succeeded Lydia Becker as leader of the constitutional movement for women's suffrage, and Emily Davies, the educationist. Many early supporters of the movement came from Unitarian or Quaker families. Members of the Bright and Cobden families (John Bright being the exception) supported women's enfranchisement. The movement was essentially middle-class, in spite of certain working-class organizations, such as the Women's Co-operative Guild, supporting the women's vote. Although the main suffrage organizations were non-party, they tended principally to attract liberal or radical backing in their early days, with the addition of some influential conservatives as time went on.[1]

The main emancipation movement gathered momentum at a time when there was something approaching a revival of puritanism. Under the influence of the Prince Consort, who was looked upon by some as a German prig, the Court set the tone and eighteenth-century laxity was discarded in favour of the new prudery. In a leading article of January 25th, 1851, *The Economist* was able to state:

> The general tone of morals in the middle and higher classes has unquestionably become much higher and purer in the last genera-

tion. Language which was common in our fathers' days would not be tolerated now. A higher sense, both of duty and of decency, has taken possession of all ranks.

The leader-writer did well to refer to 'the middle and higher classes', for the conditions under which many of the poor lived and worked made decency pretty well impossible. Although sectors of the aristocracy (in spite of the Queen's influence) and large numbers of the working-classes did not subscribe nor adhere to nineteenth-century middle-class morality, it nevertheless set the norm and had a deep and lasting effect. Perhaps the depth of the impression made was related to the coincidence of a dominant middle-class and a Queen with a middle-class, rather than aristocratic, cast of mind. Disraeli, when in doubt on popular reaction to some proposed policy or measure, was reputed to try out his ideas on the Queen, whose reaction, he found, was always typical of that of the British bourgeoisie. Even today, although we live in a so-called permissive society, with a 'pop culture' of working-class origin, the Churches and the Law Courts still largely subscribe to nineteenth-century, middle-class standards and public figures depart from this code at their peril. The mid-Victorian period seems to have been definitive of practically all aspects of our national life. Max Nicholson in his book on 'The Misgovernment of Modern Britain' concludes that 'the System' is 'basically a product of Victorian liberal thought'.[2]

The British movement was paralleled by an American movement and new light has been thrown on the connection between women's suffrage in the U.S.A. and the moral code by Alan Grimes.[3] Professor Grimes contends that the support for and early success of the women's suffrage movement in western areas was essentially related to the puritan ethic and outlook. Wyoming and Utah, as territories, enacted women's suffrage in 1869 and 1870 respectively. In the 1890s, as states, they were joined by Colorado and Idaho in including women's suffrage in their constitutions. In the U.S.A., as in this country during the nineteenth century, women's suffrage, as a goal in itself, was inadequate to attract enough support from the existing male electors to ensure success, but in the U.S.A., women's influence was associated with the traditional, puritan values, supported by the older Protestant Anglo-Saxon settlers, which were being threatened by the influx of mid-European immigrants of other faiths and, in the west, by lawless and rootless adventurers seeking gold. Women were looked upon as the bearers of civilization and had become the guardians not only of private morality, as in England, but of public morality also. Their enfranchisement was therefore supported by the Christian Temperance movement and other organizations wishing to offset the influence of the immigrants and the largely bachelor miners and adventurers by that of native-born women.

The nearest the English movement came to obtaining adventitious support was in 1884, when conservatives were inclined to favour the enfranchisement of a limited number of women of property to offset the farm labourers, colliers and Irish peasants covered by the Reform Bill of that year. On finding, after 1885, that the party could do very nicely without women's support, the idea was quietly dropped, to be revived slightly on the return of the liberals to power in December 1905. But so long as the women's enfranchisement movement in England remained constitutional, it had, in the main, to depend on the merits of its case, as seen by male electors, with a deplorably negative result.

Various forces, less conservative than those mentioned, contributed to the eventual amendment of the Federal Constitution of the U.S.A. in favour of women's suffrage in 1919, but there seems to be no doubt that the higher moral standard attributed to American women, relative to men, was largely responsible for early successes in the west, although other factors were also involved, such as the greater possibility for innovation or experiment in areas lacking constitutional traditions.

In Britain, the conventional view was that women should be the guardians of private morality and maintain the values of the home, which should be superior to those of the market-place, and thus provide a sanctuary for the men of the family. Upper- and middle-class women were allowed a measure of charitable activity, provided this did not involve them in too much publicity. It was, indeed, this charitable activity which provided some of the provocation for the claim for the vote, for those women who had the breadth of vision to see that something more than private charity was needed to tackle the social evils of the times, found, as unenfranchised persons, they were unable to exert adequate political pressure.

Englishwomen were, in some ways, less favourably placed than American women. In a more settled and civilized community, without a frontier, they were not looked upon as the guardians of civilization. Of the American West, Professor Grimes writes:

> Though men conquered the wilderness, women made it inhabitable. Women, in scarce supply in early Wyoming, were respected at the polls and in the court rooms not because they were politically equal but because they were – quite simply – women, and as such were symbols of home and civilization, whether as wives, mothers, daughters or sisters. Their very presence was in some fashion a civilizing agent.[4]

In England, women of the 'respectable classes' were respected so long as they kept to their 'proper' sphere; the courtesy shown to them was not extended to the lower classes and the presence of enormous numbers of female domestic servants, who were treated with scant respect, tended to lower the status of women generally. Servants were fair game. Steven Marcus, in his study of *The Other Victorians*, points out the nexus of sex, class and money. He discusses the extensive experience with servants enjoyed by the author of *My Secret Life*. On one occasion the author of this latter book 'had had so many gay women that I wanted a change in class . . . and began to look for a nice fresh servant'. He describes servants as follows:

> I have now had many servants in my time, and know no better companions in amorous amusements. They have rarely lost all modesty, a new lover is a treat and a fresh experience to them, even when they have had several, and few have had that.[5]

A similar attitude was taken to farm workers; the same writer reported his cousin Fred as saying, 'You can always have a field-girl; nobody cares.'[6] Interest lies in Mr Marcus's perception that many of the social assumptions of these works of Victorian pornography may also be found behind the reticences of Charles Dickens and other Victorian novelists.

Had the personal morals of the leading feminists in Britain been suspect, the successes of the latter part of the nineteenth century might well have been impeded; on the other hand, the belief that women, if enfranchised, would enforce stricter moral standards upon men, was an obstacle in the struggle for the vote. Also, it may be argued that if the effect of the women's movement had been more in the direction of emancipating society from the straitjacket of Victorian convention, reforms might have been the better attained in a generally more liberal atmosphere. Possibly those holding this view discount the effect of Josephine Butler's campaign. Although Mrs Butler and her associates were strongly opposed to loose morals, at least they tore aside the cloak of secrecy which covered the widespread commerce with prostitutes in Victorian times and through their opposition to the Contagious Diseases Acts, brought the subject of venereal disease into the arena of public discussion; it was no longer possible simply to sweep the crumbs under the carpet. Another liberalizing aspect of Josephine Butler's work was that it was a campaign to help women of the lower classes, with the result that an effective response was obtained from working-class men; this sector of the women's emancipation movement, therefore, departed from that concentration on middle-class affairs which characterized so much of the campaign.

Perhaps the women's movement had to be a middle-class one, for it was middle-class, restrictive Victorian attitudes which were essentially 'the enemy'. Through the women's campaign the dominance of the husband and father came under fire, but the respectable woman was left on her uncomfortable pedestal, which she was prepared to share with her spouse, rather than find a more comfortable place for the two of them at a slightly lower level. With hindsight, one cannot help wishing that some leading English feminists had challenged not only the double moral standard but also the idea that chastity was the only and overriding virtue so far as women were concerned; but the feminists might well have retorted that it was only their personal probity and high moral standards which enabled them to achieve what they did.

Obviously a certain variety of attitudes towards moral problems must have been contained in a movement as extensive and with as many facets as the women's emancipation movement, but typical of attitudes held were the opinions of Millicent Garrett Fawcett. As Millicent Garrett, she was too young to join her sister Elizabeth and Emily Davies in taking the 1866 women's petition for the vote to the Houses of Parliament; in 1928, after years of leadership of the constitutional movement for women's suffrage, she survived to witness the equalization of the franchise.

In 1891, a year short of the centenary of the publication of Mary Wollstonecraft's *A Vindication of the Rights of Woman*, a new edition of this book was brought out, to which Mrs Fawcett contributed an Introduction. By this time Mary Wollstonecraft was thoroughly rehabilitated. It was no longer a sin to have been a Jacobin. Nevertheless, amongst much praise of Mary Wollstonecraft's ideas, the following passage occurs:

> There are other faults . . . which are probably to be traced to a reaction against the school of ethics, which proclaimed that appearances and decorum were ends in themselves to be diligently sought for. To this reaction may also, I believe, be attributed the errors of Mary Wollstonecraft's own life, and those of so many members of the circle in which she moved. In unravelling the curious tangle of relationships, intrigues, suicides and attempted suicides of the remarkable group of personalities to whom Mary Wollstonecraft belonged, one is sickened for ever, as Mr. Matthew Arnold has said, of the subject of irregular relations.[7]

This extract shows that certain basic attitudes were held by the writer: the conventional condemnation of Mary Wollstonecraft's irregular association with Imlay, a lack of sympathy with the desperate straits which could bring a woman to attempt suicide and an implication (though this may not have been intended) that Mary Wollstonecraft was in some way responsible for the irregular affairs of her family which occurred after her death (see Chapter 2). Mrs Fawcett goes on to praise her subject for believing that a higher concept of womanhood was possible within the framework of women's marital duties: 'Mary Wollstonecraft's great merit, however, lies in this, that . . . she did not sanction any deprecation of the immense importance of the domestic duties of women.'[8]

This is the point at which the modern feminist would quarrel with Mrs Fawcett's attitude, holding that emancipation is impossible without some modification of traditional domestic patterns. The problem, as modern women are apt to see it, is to adjust family life and lessen domestic duties without a deterioration in the quality of life and the care of children. Most would probably contend that the present-day sharing of domestic responsibilities between husband, wife and children, without a rigid division of function, makes for an improved quality of family life, and certainly marriage is more popular than ever before and we are an increasingly 'home-centred' society. A few would perhaps have the courage to agree with Edmund Leach in his refusal to support the 'sacred cow' of the close-knit family. According to Professor Leach:

> The parents and children huddled together in their loneliness take too much out of each other. The parents fight; the children rebel. Children need to grow up in larger, more relaxed domestic groups centred on the community rather than on mother's kitchen. . . [9]

To revert to Mrs Fawcett, she quotes Mary Wollstonecraft as praising 'marriage as the foundation of almost every social virtue' and attributes to Mary's initiative the fact that, in England, the women's rights movement had 'kept free from the excesses and follies that in some other countries have marred its course'.[10] In the twentieth century, the suffragettes were to attribute the lack of success of the constitutional movement in obtaining the vote to its conventionality and timidity; they were to indulge in excesses deplored by Mrs Fawcett and her associates.

Later in this same introduction, Mrs Fawcett expresses her dislike of the prevalent double standard of morality and praises Mary Wollstonecraft for her opposition to this. Mrs Fawcett's attitude is again typical:

> Unchastity in men means unchastity in women; and the cure for the ills which unchastity brings with it is not to be found in penitentiaries and in Magdalen institutions, but in a truer measure of justice as regards the responsibilities of both sexes, in opening to women a variety of honourable means of earning a living, and in developing in men and women self-government and a sense of their responsibility to each other, themselves, their children and the nation.[11]

In other words, Mrs Fawcett wanted men and women to live up to conventional moral standards; she wished to change behaviour, not the standards. G. E. Mowry's comment on the American movement applied equally to Britain: 'What they [the feminists] wanted was equality, but an equality based upon a standard of feminine virtue instead of masculine sin.'[12]

Men who, in protection of their property rights, had prevailed upon society to accept a high and exacting standard of female virtue, had eventually fashioned a rod for their own backs.

Mrs Fawcett was writing before the world became a 'global village' and in view of the prevailing cultural atmosphere, one can understand (but cannot help becoming impatient with) the attitude taken by her and by Emily Davies that their cherished movements must not be tainted by any breath of scandal. Millicent Fawcett was afraid that the odium of Josephine Butler's campaign would rub off on to the suffrage movement and Emily Davies feared that the detestation which the struggle for the vote evoked would affect her efforts to storm the stronghold of higher education. The controversy occasioned by the campaign against the Contagious Diseases Acts split the suffrage movement in two in 1871, for Josephine Butler was a supporter of women's suffrage and a sector of the London Society (which became known as the Old London Committee) felt there should be a 'careful avoidance of even apparent mingling with any other agitation', and that 'no person conspicuously engaged either as officer or lecturer in some other agitations now proceeding, to which we will not further allude, should hold any conspicuous place in the movement for women's suffrage'. Reunion between the two groups was not achieved until 1877.

Emily Davies opened a women's college at Hitchin, rather than Cambridge, in 1869, as she thought it would be disastrous to let her girls loose in a university town and that the slightest breath of scandal would put an end to her plans for a genuine university course. The girls were carefully chaperoned and restricted in a way which came to irritate many of them and which was unsuitable for young women trained to think for themselves, but to Emily Davies, who had fought so fiercely for her cause, everything had to be sacrificed to the main objective; no unnecessary grounds for criticism should be provided, even if this involved a certain amount of humbug.

No hint of free love besmirched the record of the mainstream of the British feminist movement. Charity for 'unfortunates' – yes! But parallel with the desire for equality and social justice was the belief that women's emancipation would lead to a more elevated social order, judged by Victorian moral standards. The atheists, socialists and others who supported the women's cause but challenged conventional morality were not included in the main-stream.

In the U.S.A., where the feminists' association with high moral standards had contributed to early successes in the west, the question arose, in 1872, whether to take advantage of the position which Victoria Woodhull (1838–1927) had carved out for herself (not without male assistance). Mrs Woodhull, who, with her sister, Tennie, had already stormed the male stronghold of Wall Street by acting as a stockbroker, was claiming the right to be nominated for the presidency of the U.S.A. She had (again, with masculine help) drawn up a Memorial on the interpretation of the Constitution and was allowed to address the Judiciary Committee of the House of Representatives on January 11th, 1872, on the subject of her Memorial. Obviously this was a situation which could be capitalized by the suffrage societies but, alas, Mrs Woodhull's name was associ-ated with scandalous rumours. Had she not been living in a house which contained both her current and former husband? Did she not claim the right to free love? Was she not closely associated with her sister, Tennessee (Tennie), whose morals could only be described as easy? At the time, the American movement for women's suffrage was split in two, the less conservative branch, the National Woman Suffrage Association, rising nobly to the challenge, after much heart-searching, and backing Victoria. Elizabeth Cady Stanton, one of the leaders of the N.W.S.A., counter-attacked the puritans:

> We have had enough women sacrificed to this sentimental, hypo-critical prating about purity. . . . This is one of man's most effective engines for our division and subjugation. He creates the public sentiment, builds the gallows, and then makes us hangmen for our sex. We have crucified the Mary Wollstonecrafts, the Fanny Wrights, the Georges Sands, the Fanny Kembles, of all ages. . . . Let us end this ignoble record. . . . If Victoria Woodhull must be crucified, let men drive the spikes and plait the crown of thorns.[13]

One looks in vain for similar sentiments within the mainstream of the English women's emancipation movement.

3 A Night House—Kate Hamilton's *From Henry Mayhew's 'London Labour and the London Poor'*

4 The Haymarket—Midnight *From Henry Mayhew's 'London Labour and the London Poor'*

Notes

1 Cf. Rover, Constance, *Women's Suffrage and Party Politics in Britain, 1866–1914,* 1967, for a full analysis of the politics of the suffrage campaign.

2 Nicholson, Max, *The System,* 1967, 498.

3 Grimes, Alan, *The Puritan Ethic and Woman Suffrage,* 1967.

4 *Ibid.,* 76.

5 Marcus, Steven, *The Other Victorians,* 1966, 133.

6 *Ibid.,* 137.

7 Fawcett, Millicent Garrett, Introduction to Wollstonecraft, Mary, *A Vindication of the Rights of Woman,* 1891, 22–3.

8 *Ibid.,* 23.

9 Leach, Edmund, 'Ourselves and Others', in *The Listener,* 30.11.1967, 695, col. 3.

10 Fawcett, *op. cit.,* 23.

11 *Ibid.,* 27.

12 Mowry, G. E., *The Era of Theodore Roosevelt,* 1962, 36. See also Grimes, *op. cit.,* 104.

13 Johnston, Johanna, *Mrs Satan,* 1967, 92.

8

The Invisible Society

One more Unfortunate,
  Weary of breath,
Rashly importunate,
  Gone to her death!

Thomas Hood

Before considering Josephine Butler's emergence as a heroine of the
women's movement, on account of her successful campaign against
the Contagious Diseases Acts, it is necessary to look at the shady
side of the Victorian scene and consider 'the great social evil',
as the contemporary euphemism ran.

Numerical evidence on the extent of prostitution is necessarily
lacking; a Thames Police Court magistrate estimated there were
50,000 prostitutes in London at the beginning of the nineteenth
century, while the Bishop of Exeter suggested 80,000, as did a Mr
Talbot, secretary of the Society for the Protection of Young
Females. Police returns, based on the occupancy of certain brothels
and lodging-houses in the Metropolitan Police District, show that
9,409 prostitutes were known to the police in 1841, 8,600 in 1857
and 6,515 in 1868, but William Acton, who quotes these figures,
stated 'these returns give but a faint idea of the grand total of prostitution'.[1] One cannot but agree with Thomas Huxley's comment on
the statistics quoted by supporters of the Contagious Diseases Acts
as 'utterly unreliable and worthless'; nevertheless, prostitution was
obviously extensive and there were special features in the Victorian
social and economic situation which contributed to its prevalence
in London and other cities, garrison towns and sea-ports. An examination of the social context cannot, of course, explain why one
woman becomes a prostitute while another, similarly situated, does

not, but it may throw some light on a situation where it was obviously worthwhile for the prostitute to make an open display of her attractions, and also partially illuminate that somewhat shadowy figure, the prostitute's client. While social conditions do not explain everything, it would be folly to ignore them.

The subject of prostitution in Victorian times was investigated by William Acton, a surgeon with experience both in London and Paris, who, writing in the mid-century, asked the question:

> Who are those fair creatures, neither chaperons nor chaperoned,
> 'Those somebodies whom nobody knows', who elbow our wives and
> daughters in the parks and promenades and rendezvous of fashion?
> Who are these painted dressy women, flaunting along the streets
> and boldly accosting the passers-by? Who are those miserable
> creatures, ill-fed, ill-clothed, uncared for, from whose misery the eye
> recoils, cowering under dark arches and among bye-lanes?[2]

Prostitution seemed to become more blatant as the century progressed. *The Pall Mall Gazette*, on April 16th, 1869, reported:

The Ladies' Mile

> Although up to this period of the season the people who ride or
> drive in the Row have not been distracted by any specially sensa-
> tional ponies under the direction of anonymous ladies, questionable
> broughams and horsebreakers have even thus early appeared in
> Hyde Park in excess of the number with which the assemblage is
> usually enlivened. . . . Until very recently there was no such thing
> as a demi-monde in London . . . but within a very brief period –
> not much more than a year, perhaps – there has been a change
> amongst us. Previous to that time . . . moralists in the press com-
> plained of the frank terms which young men of fashion held with
> such women in places of public resort. This familiarity is so much
> on the increase, (as any one who watches what goes on in the Ladies'
> Mile can perceive) that it calls for some remonstrance. Formerly
> Aspasia and her associates were passed with a nod, or only spoken
> to by men who were indifferent to notice because they were them-
> selves unknown, or, at any rate, if they recognized such women they
> were cautious where it was done. At present the . . . denizens of St
> Johns Wood and Pimlico are chatted with as candidly as if they had
> come up from some dove-cote in the country. . . . A notion seems
> to prevail that the loose women . . . are indistinguishable from the

women of virtue. . . . In the Park, at least, there is no difficulty in guessing the occupation of the dashing *equestrienne* who salutes half-a-dozen men at once with her whip or with a wink, and who sometimes varies the monotony of a safe seat by holding her hands behind her back while gracefully swerving over to listen to the compliments of a walking admirer.[3]

There were social factors affecting both the demand for and supply of prostitutes. To take the demand side first, 'the Joneses' were with the Victorians as they are with us today; the Victorian period was materialistic; young people of the middle-classes expected to start married life where their parents left off and genteel poverty was despised by society. In order to make a prudent marriage, the bridegroom needed to be in a position to maintain not only himself and his wife, but a succession of children which might arrive at annual intervals and the necessary domestic staff to maintain such a household – not to mention a carriage for his wife, so that the family might be classed as 'carriage folk'. All this tended to make young men delay marriage or, in some instances, finding themselves comfortable at their clubs or with other unofficial arrangements, reject it altogether. A letter to *The Times* of May 7th, 1857, signed by 'Theophrastus', complained of this state of affairs:

The laws which society imposes in the present day in respect of marriage upon young men belonging to the middle-class are, in the highest degree, unnatural, and are the real cause of most of our social corruptions. The father of a family has, in many instances, risen from a comparatively humble origin to a position of easy competence. His wife has her carriage; he associates with men of wealth greater than his own. His sons reach the age when, in the natural course of things they ought to marry and establish a home for themselves. . . . The son must not marry until he can maintain an establishment on much the same footing as his father's. If he dare to set the law at defiance, his family lost *caste* and he and his wife are quietly dropped out of the circle in which they have hitherto moved. All that society will allow is an engagement, and then we have the sad but familiar sight of two young lovers wearing out their best years with hearts sickened with hope long deferred; often, after all, ending in disappointment, or in the shattered health of the poor girl, unable to bear up against the harassing anxiety. . . . But stay awhile, society. Your picture of marriage at 35, with a

Belgravian house for the happy couple, a footman in splendid uniform, and at least a brougham, is very pleasing; but there is a reverse to the canvas, and that is a very dark one. How has the bridegroom been living since he attained his manhood? . . . I know there are thousands who are living in sin, chiefly in consequence of the impossibility (as the world says) of their marrying. Living in the midst of temptation, they have not sufficient principle to resist its fascination . . . yet they dare not offend their family, alienate their friends, and lose their social position by making what the world calls an imprudent marriage.

. . . the fact is . . . that with regard to some things, and among them marriage, there is a numerous and increasing class, by no means the waifs and strays of the community, who are disposed, not to question or propose any change in the law, but simply to ignore it, and to 'put up', as they say, 'with the consequences'.[4]

The anti-matrimonial tendencies of the day reduced certain society matrons to despair, and seven Belgravian mothers wrote to *The Times* in June 1861, complaining of the situation. They described the careful upbringing and launching of their daughters and the varied and attractive dispositions of the girls, some of whom had been in London society for as long as seven seasons, adding:

We 7 have at this moment 24 daughters, actually what our sons call 'in running', not one of them has had an offer that any one of us mothers for a moment could have seriously entertained. We offer a supply of that which ought to be to the nobility of our day, what cotton is to Manchester, but all demand has ceased. . . . However unpleasant, indelicate the truth . . . marriage in our set is voted a bore – is repudiated. . . . there is in existence a rule of life which won't even hear of marriage . . . an openly recognised anti-matrimonial element pervades good society. The just privileges of our daughters are set aside; the 'heirs' dance with them, flirt with them, dine with us, shoot our game, drink our claret, but they will not marry. And why? Because what our simple-minded daughters call 'the pretty horsebreakers' occupy naughtily and temporarily where we should occupy *en permanence*.

Go where we will, the mother's eye has this social cruel pest intruded upon it; these bad rivals of our children are no longer kept in the background. . . . Neither Row nor ring, church nor chapel, opera nor concert are wanting in their evident, recognized presence.

Our husbands have been at their 'balls' – the best dancing, they say, and perfect decorum. In short, 'establishments' reign; our children seem condemned to live and die either unestablished, or to be given away at last as wives to people of limited means and no position. Time was, Sir, when a Lawrence, and then a Grant, placed on the walls of the Royal Exhibition lovely pictures each season of daughters now first offered to the attention of England's fashionable world. . . . The picture of the year is a 'Pretty Horsebreaker' – but too well-known. . . .

It is said . . . that by making heavy settlements so imperative we drove younger sons to the evil life which was comparatively cheap . . . that we, by encouraging the 'heirs' whose 'horsebreakers' were notorious sanctioned the sin that we might catch the sinners, and thus confirmed them in their non-marriage life. . . .

And then the sin of it all!

A Sorrowing Mother for Seven of them.[5]

This lament provoked a reply from a man signing himself *Beau Jolais*, describing how the extravagant expectation of his proposed wife caused him to give up the prospect of matrimony. The letter was headed 'Horsebreakers and Heartbreakers' and included the following paragraphs:

The matrons of Belgravia point angrily to those whom they designate as 'the pretty horsebreakers' who cluster amid the shady retreats of Brompton, or dwell among the calm groves of the Evangelist. These frail young beings are, however, not the cause, but rather the result, of the circumstances so feelingly described and so deeply deplored.

In the room at this club where I am now writing there are 15 men similarly engaged . . . they have been reluctantly compelled to follow my example.

Girls . . . are now so expensively, so thoughtlessly, brought up – are led to expect so lavish an outlay on the part of the husband, that, unless his means are unlimited, he must, to comply with the wishes of a modern wife, soon bring himself to beggary. Hence it is that hundreds have been forced to abandon all notion of a connubial alliance, taking up instead with a simpler and more economical arrangement, temporary or permanent as the case may be. . . .

Respectability may be too dearly purchased.

Far be it from me to deny that extravagance enough is to be encountered even among the ranks of the 'horsebreakers'; but it is a mistake to suppose that there are not many among them who possess tact and art enough to retain permanently in their possession young hearts that would have fondly beaten responsively to a far holier attachment had not the cold frown of a too zealous matchmaker sternly forbidden the bans, thus excluding the unfortunate victim from a higher and more ennobling career.

Queen of Clubs, June 27   Beau Jolais[6]

Turning to less elevated sectors of society, the married establishment of the army was limited by regulation and, in any event, a soldier must have completed seven years' service and be in possession of at least one good conduct badge, before he could apply for permission to marry. The result was that 93 soldiers out of every 100 were unmarried.

Compared with the middle-classes, working-class men married early but many such marriages broke down through poverty, leaving the men footloose and the women to fend for themselves.

The situation was, therefore, that a great many men, for one reason or another, were not in a position to obtain legitimate satisfaction of their sexual needs and, with temptation all around them, were not inclined to lead celibate lives. In the middle- and upper-classes, the prevailing moral code and strict supervision of unmarried girls made it necessary for the Victorian man to step outside his own class for pre-marital experience. The demand for illicit intercourse was not, of course, restricted to single men and it was necessary and convenient, also, for the married, middle-class man, wishing for extramarital experience, to seek it in the class beneath him. The temptations of the married man were added to by the refusal of society to consider the 'good' woman capable of sexual enjoyment and expertise. The devil, apparently, had all the fun as well as the best tunes.

On the supply side, contributory factors were the excess of women over men in all adult age groups and the bitter poverty to be found amongst working-class women. Males were subject to a higher death-rate than females, particularly in infancy and childhood; the Victorian improvements in public health affected females, with their somewhat greater capacity for survival, more than males, and accidental death was more liable to affect men, with their activity in dangerous trades, than women. Emigration and service overseas were much commoner amongst men than women. In 1851 statistics show that as great a proportion of women, relative to the population as a whole, was working as was the case in 1951, but as opportunities for employment were limited, women were crowded into relatively few occupations, with the inevitable effect of depressing the level of wages and providing employers with opportunities for 'sweating' their workers. A respectable young woman in London in the mid-nineteenth century could find herself unable to earn more than 3s to 5s a week, even if she worked from early morning to late at night. Conditions were so bad in many trades that the workers' health broke down within a few years, so that the only recourse was the streets. London seamstresses, for instance, were expected to work practically night and day on rush orders at the height of the London season, in unhealthy, ill-ventilated rooms, and they frequently turned consumptive.

The supply of prostitutes was linked to the low status of women, their lack of opportunity in obtaining employment at all, due in part to lack of education and training, and the low level of wages when work could be obtained. The low pay of certain classes of men also affected the situation, many a soldier's wife going 'on the town' through inability to exist on the beggarly allowance provided by the army.

The traditional road to ruin in Victorian England was a girl's seduction, followed by the arrival of an illegitimate child. This meant loss of 'character', making it practically impossible to obtain employment in the overcrowded labour market. As one maid-servant who had lost her character put it, the only Madam who would engage a servant without a character was – a Madam!

Another source of supply was from that social group to be found in the cities and known as 'the criminal classes'. In some slum areas it was practically inevitable that the men should grow up to be thieves and the women prostitutes. In Victorian times, as indeed, in other periods, large numbers of men and women were living on their wits, particularly in the cities. From this sector of society came the large number of juvenile prostitutes which infested the streets of London and upon which foreign visitors often made unfavourable comments. Prior to 1875, the age of consent was 12.

The above factors must be looked upon as causes of prostitution additional to those which obtain today. We are not really sure what makes women turn to prostitution in the age of the welfare state, but reasons are thought to include the desire for easy money, dislike of the monotonous work which is sometimes all that is available for untrained women, personal psychological difficulties, possibly stemming from childhood experiences, and, in a certain proportion of cases, a low level of intelligence bordering on mental deficiency.

The Wolfenden Report suggests that most prostitutes are 'women whose psychological make-up is such that they choose this life because they find in it a style of living which is to them easier, freer and more profitable than would be provided by any other occupation',[7] and Edward Glover states: 'Prostitution exhibits regressive characteristics; it represents a primitive phase in sexual development. It is a kind of sexual backwardness.'[8] He looks upon economic factors as ancillary only and deems the causes of prostitution to be essentially psychological.[9] Common ground with the Victorians is that even in the more permissive climate of today, and in spite of a viable alternative, the birth of an illegitimate child may be a preliminary to a woman taking to prostitution.

The picture of Victorian times which emerges is that prostitution was an integral part of the economy; to have removed it would have been like abstracting a whole trade or occupation, such as factory work, from the trades followed by women. As well as destitution being a cause of prostitution, the picture can be looked at the other way round; there would have been far more destitution amongst women than was actually the case if they had not been able to resort to prostitution. There was something in the maxim that 'morals fluctuate with trade'.

The Victorian image was that of the continual and rapid descent of the prostitute to an early grave. According to William Logan, a missionary in the slums of Glasgow:

The tendency is always downwards . . . rising is a thing unknown. It cannot be. It is all descent. Whether seduced in private, or beguiled into one of the superior receptacles of infamy it is seldom long ere satiety and the passion for change throw her [the prostitute] off. She is turned mercilessly adrift. . . . It is all down – down – rapidly down, till it terminates in some such scene of squalid wretchedness as the one just depicted.[10]

The 'scene of squalid wretchedness' was drawn from the *Westminster Review* and one cannot help feeling that it was quoted with a measure of relish:

> There comes the last sad scene of all, when drink, disease and starvation have laid her on her death-bed. On a wretched pallet in a filthy garret, with no companions but the ruffians, drunkards and harlots with whom she had cast in her lot; amid brutal curses, ribald language and drunken laughter; with a past – which, even were there no future, would be dreadful to contemplate – laying its weight of despair upon her soul; with a prospective beyond the grave which the little she retains of her early religion lights up for her with the lurid light of hell, – this poor daughter of humanity terminates a life, of which, if the sin has been grievous and the weakness lamentable, the expiation has been fearfully tremendous.[11]

Dr Acton's thorough investigation of the subject, recorded in the two editions of his book published in 1857 and 1870, showed that this picture simply was not true in the generality of cases and that prostitution was 'a transitory state through which an untold number of British women were ever on their passage'. Josephine Butler, who also made extensive investigations, concurred with this view.

Acton rejected the contention that the prostitute always met a miserable death and insisted:

> If we compare the prostitute at 35 with her sister, who perhaps is the married mother of a family, or has been a toiling slave for years in the over-heated laboratories of fashion, we shall seldom find that the constitutional ravages often thought to be necessary consequences of prostitution exceed those attributable to the cares of a family and the heart-wearing struggles of virtuous labour.[12]

He also quoted French evidence, to the effect that:

> Their [prostitutes'] health resists all attacks better than that of the ordinary run of women who have children and lead orderly lives. They have (as someone has remarked) iron bodies, which enable them with impunity to meet trials such as would prove fatal to others.[13]

Admittedly prostitutes suffered from what might be termed occupational diseases, but so did many groups of women workers. For instance, match-girls with Bryant & May (who were no worse than other employers) suffered from necrosis of the jaw (phossy-jaw), which caused their teeth to drop out. This was the result of inhaling the fumes of chemicals.

Dr Acton's investigations led to the conclusion that a surprising number of prostitutes married and subsequently led regular lives; others saved money and bought a shop, or a lodging-house. Some, in their turn, exploited younger prostitutes and ran brothels and other disorderly establishments; these, however, were a minority and most became assimilated with the ordinary population.

The point Acton was trying to make was that prostitutes were not a group set apart from the rest of the community, whose welfare could be ignored. He pointed out that many prostitutes were mothers when they commenced their career and many more raised families after abandoning prostitution. He wished to see, amongst other reforms, some changes in the bastardy laws, so that the mothers of illegitimate children had some alternative to going on the streets, and felt it wrong that society should place the whole responsibility for the upbringing of an illegitimate child upon the mother. As already mentioned (see Chapter 6) the maximum sum which could be obtained from the father, if paternity were established in the courts, was half-a-crown a week until the child reached the age of thirteen; orders were frequently made for lesser sums, such as 1s 6d or 2s.

If we now turn, briefly, to Victorian attitudes and what the Victorians tried to do about prostitution, we find that most of them, though deploring it, would have preferred to ignore the fact. Religious organizations set up penitentiaries to try to rehabilitate some of the women, but, by all accounts, these were cheerless places and scarcely an advertisement for the virtuous life. Another sector of the community looked upon prostitution as the safety-valve of society, shielding virtuous women from temptation. W. E. H. Lecky, in his well-known statement in the *History of European Morals* (1869), praised the prostitute as 'the most efficient guardian of virtue', without whom 'the unchallenged purity of countless happy homes would be polluted'.[14]

A modern criticism of Victorian sexual attitudes is provided by Dr Fernando Henriques:

> In our opinion Victorian sexual morality represents a reaction against the libertinism of the Regency. It was a morality which fostered prurience and hypocrisy. From the stronghold of the chaste, mono-gamous family it enabled the individual to fulminate against all vicious living while clandestinely he sowed his wild oats. It encouraged wives to become sexual ninnies while their husbands contracted venereal disease. It hounded 'fallen' women to become whores in the name of God. Fear and Evangelicalism must bear the responsibility.[15]

The demand for prostitutes is unlikely to disappear and is liable to continue to be met; deprivation is relative and the modern counter-part of a woman who, in Victorian times, resorted to prostitution in order to exist might well be one who prefers to earn in a night as much as she could earn in a week by 'honest' labour.

The Victorian feminists over-emphasized the economic motive behind prostitution, assuming that few would resort to it if an honest living were possible. The economic motive has been disputed by several authorities, including Havelock Ellis. The argument runs that with better wages and fuller employment for women, the price a prostitute could obtain would rise, therefore the calling would be correspondingly more attractive. Havelock Ellis, contended that the great number of servants recruited to prostitution contradicted the argument that it was largely occasioned by destitution, as servants at least had bed and board.[16] However, one does not know how many of these servants had lost their 'character'. Present-day experience supports Ellis's contention, as 'the social evil' is still with us in the welfare state.

Dr Henriques, in his work cited above, tends to argue that prostitution is governed by demand. While not disputing that there is a permanent, hard core of demand, demand is useless without at least a latent supply. It is not much use demanding the harvest which has failed. The ample and obvious supply of prostitutes in Victorian times did much to sustain demand; attractive shop-windows lead to impulse buying; but, of course, demand and supply interact. It seems reasonable to assume that since those days the supply has been decreased by those governed (at least in part) by actual or near destitution rather than by less pardonable or more obscure motives. There have been changes, also, on the demand side, for many of the causes, such as late marriage or fear of unwanted pregnancy, which made the Victorian middle-class man go outside his own social circle or away from his own wife, have largely disappeared. A note of caution is necessary, however, for the Wolfenden Report states: 'We have no reliable evidence whether the number of prostitutes plying their trade in the streets of London has changed significantly in recent years.'[17]

Also, since that date, the call-girl has to some extent replaced the street-walker in Britain, as a result of the Street Offences Act of 1959, and the motor-car has provided a way of circumventing the difficulties the law has placed in the way of those wishing to obtain accommodation for the purpose of prostitution. A broadcast on September 22nd, 1968, mentioned a police estimate of 10,000 prostitutes in London's West End, which is not far from the 9,409 known to the police in 1841, though presumably a wider area is now served. These figures, however, are very different from the 80,000 mentioned by the Bishop of Exeter at the beginning of the century and the 80,000 referred to by Keir Hardie 'on good authority'[18] as being on the streets of London at the time of the Piccadilly Flats case (1913) (see Chapter 16). The nature of the subject is such that it is impossible to obtain reliable statistics. (The broadcast referred to, on Radio 4, was entitled: *Subject for Sunday: The True Sex Life of the Average British Male*. One wonders why this was thought a more suitable subject for Sunday than for Saturday night.)

What the nineteenth-century feminists had to fight was a climate of opinion in the 'establishment' which held that prostitution was necessary, therefore there was little point in doing anything about it apart from trying to check the drain on public funds occasioned by disease in the armed forces. Brothel-keeping was not a statutory offence until 1885, although there was a Disorderly Houses Act of 1871 which applied to London. The common law on the subject was mainly related to the abatement of nuisance. Vested interests played their part in the *laissez-faire* attitude adopted, for the brewers and publicans in many urban areas, particularly sea-ports, benefited from the presence of the 'ladies of the town'. Prostitution encouraged drinking and drinking encouraged prostitution. An obvious way to limit the evil, which has since proved effective, was through the strict control of the liquor trade.

As always, the evils of under-privilege were interrelated; an attack on all fronts against the inferior position of women was necessary before much could be done for the masses of uneducated, untrained women, for whom the economy had no recognized place. The cushion of the welfare state was needed before it became possible to examine the prostitute in the context of social deviance, rather than that of destitution.

Notes

1 Acton, William, *Prostitution considered in its Moral, Social and Sanitary Aspects in London and Other Large Cities and Garrison Towns with Proposals for the Control and Prevention of its Attendant Evils*, 1870, 176.

2 *Ibid.*, viii of Preface.

3 *Pall Mall Gazette*, 16.4.1869, 5.

4 Letter to *The Times*, 'The Other Side of the Picture', 7.5.1857, 12, col. 6.

5 Letter to *The Times*, 27.6.1861, 6, col. 4.

6 Letter to *The Times*, 28.6.1861, 12, col. 5.

7 H.M.S.O., *Report of the Committee on Homosexual Offences and Prostitution*, 1957, 79, Cmnd. 247, 79, para. 223.

8 Glover, Edward, *The Psychology of Prostitution*, 1957, 8. Originally delivered as a lecture at a meeting convened by the International Bureau for the Suppression of Traffic in Women and Children.

9 *Ibid.*, 14–15.

10 Logan, William, *The Great Social Evil*, 1871, 104.

11 *Ibid.*

12 Acton, *op. cit.*, 39.

13 *Ibid.*

14 Lecky, W. E. H., *History of European Morals*, 1905, ii. 283.

15 Henriques, Fernando, *Modern Sexuality: Prostitution and Society*, 1968, iii. 231.

16 Ellis, Havelock, *Studies in the Psychology of Sex*, 1911, vi. 259–66.

17 Note 7, *op. cit.*, 82, para. 230.

18 H.C. Deb., 5S, Vol. LVI, c. 2,341.

9

Josephine Butler
and the Contagious Diseases Acts

Most unfortunately, though from the very best motives –
the desire to prevent public discussion on a subject not
fit for proper discussion – these [Contagious Diseases]
Acts were passed almost without the knowledge of anyone.

Gladstone (House of Commons, May 7th, 1883)

The Victorians, like ourselves, were apt to set up Select Committees
and Royal Commissions on troublesome matters and then to do
little about their reports. One development, however, spurred them
to action and that was the high level of venereal disease in the army
and navy and consequent drain on the public purse. A committee of
the House of Lords gave as an example that in the year 1860, 'one
in four of the foot guards in London suffered from syphilis'.[1]
Contagious Diseases Acts were passed, therefore, in 1864, 1866 and
1869 with the object of checking the spread of disease within the
armed forces.

The first Act applied to eleven military stations, garrisons and
sea-port towns and provided for the surgical examination of
prostitutes thought to be diseased, their detention in hospital if
diseased and the punishment of brothel-keepers who knowingly
harboured diseased prostitutes. It was subsequently admitted by
the Royal Commission upon the Administration of the Contagious
Diseases Acts, reporting in 1871, that 'This (1864) Act passed
without much notice either in or out of Parliament' (C. 408, para. 1).
It was not administered by the local police but by officers drawn
from the Metropolitan Police.

The Act of 1866 repealed that of 1864 but re-enacted its provisions with a certain tightening up. Instead of applying only to
prostitutes thought to be diseased, it provided for the periodical

examination of all prostitutes within the prescribed districts and for
the detention of those found to be diseased on the certificate of the
examining surgeon, without the order of a magistrate. The Act of
1869 enlarged the provisions and extended the operation of the
1866 Act, including eighteen towns within its scope. Referring to
these two latter Acts, the Royal Commission reported: 'The Act of
1866 was little heeded amid the party strife and the agitation of
questions of the highest political importance which marked that
year. The Act of 1869, which amended and extended the Act of
1866, also passed without opposition' (C. 408, para. 16).

It seems incredible that our vaunted, constitutional safeguards
of debate in two Houses of Parliament went for nothing and one
wonders how the Acts were smuggled through. Apparently very
few M.P.s realized what was happening, as the Government took
the stages of the bills last thing at night, when most of the members
had gone home, or at the end of the session. The entries in the
indices of the appropriate volumes of *Hansard* are studded with
asterisks. The explanatory note reads as follows: 'When in Index a
* is added to the Reading of a Bill, it indicates that no Debate took
place upon that Stage of the measure.'

The House of Lords, which claimed to be 'the watchdog of the
people', passed the measures through without debate, in spite of the
fact that they robbed a sector of the population of their civil liberties
and introduced a system of police spies. The story has it (for which
the writer does not vouch) that Queen Victoria, in giving the Royal
Assent, thought the Acts were extensions of Contagious Diseases
of Cattle Acts which had previously been passed.

The method of implementing the Acts locally was in a similarly
underhand manner. In 1870 a Mrs Kell, wife of a Unitarian minister,
told the Royal Commissioners who were investigating the working
of the Contagious Diseases Acts: 'I think it was nearly a month after
they [the Contagious Diseases Acts] were in action before many
people in Southampton knew they were in action there. They were
smuggled into the town, I may say' (C. 408–1, 2n. 16860).

Eventually, because of the opposition aroused when at length
the public realized what had happened, the House of Commons
debated the matter behind closed doors, Jacob Bright (brother of
John Bright) speaking as follows on July 20th, 1870:

Poor men's houses are entered, women suspected of incontinence, but who are in no sense common prostitutes, are forced into this vile slavery. . . . Here is a law passed by peers and prelates in one chamber, and by an assembly of rich men in another, the whole burden of which is directed against the poor women of the country. It is the most indefensible piece of class legislation of which I have any knowledge. How are these Acts carried out? Their victims are not brought to Court and fairly judged. There is provision by which they can be made to sign what is called a voluntary submission. Women frightened by the police are induced to sign their names or put their crosses to a paper of the meaning of which they know nothing. Every kind of cajolery and fraud are resorted to to obtain the signature of ignorant and defenceless women. Then once they have committed themselves they are subjected to forced examinations every fortnight and have upon them a brand which makes a return to decent life almost impossible.[2]

Because of her selfless work amongst the prostitutes of Liverpool, Josephine Butler was called upon to lead a campaign for the repeal of the Contagious Diseases Acts. She was a thorough-going feminist and an active supporter of women's education, married women's right to separate property and women's suffrage. After much heart-searching, and with her husband's support, she agreed to oppose the Acts, thus bringing upon her head the fury of the conventional sector of society, which took the attitude that it was a greater evil to bring the facts of prostitution to light than to ignore its existence. In particular, it was thought that respectable women should know nothing about such matters. A Ladies' National Association for the Repeal of the Contagious Diseases Acts was founded in 1869 (following the formation of the National Association for the Abolition of the Contagious Diseases Acts) and on December 31st of that year their members' protest appeared in the *Daily News*; signatories included Harriet Martineau, Florence Nightingale, Mary Carpenter and many well-known women belonging to the Society of Friends.

The basis of the attack on the Acts was that certain women were being robbed of their civil rights and the Constitution was consequently being violated. It was also alleged that the Acts provided for the state regulation of vice, and therefore gave to it an implied condonation. It was held that wide discretionary powers were given to the police, which imperilled the innocent as well as the guilty, and that the Acts were directed against the poorer classes. In addition, it was contended that the Acts failed in their purpose of checking disease; this latter point (which could well have been pressed home, especially in view of continental experience) was looked upon by Mrs Butler and her friends as relatively unimportant compared with the moral issues involved. Lastly, but not least, prostitutes were being regulated but not their customers, thus perpetuating the double moral standard.

The motive for the passing of the Acts was the straightforward one of protecting the health of the armed forces, but, under attack, supporters were forced to consider the prostitutes as well as the servicemen and moved to other arguments, such as that reformatory work was undertaken while women were compulsorily detained in hospital, that the women increased in self-respect, cleanliness and appearance as well as in health. In short, a belated effort was made to prove that the Acts were for the benefit of the prostitutes as well as their customers. Defendants of the Acts were apt to tie themselves in knots, trying to explain how, at one and the same time, prostitution was checked and better and healthier prostitutes were produced.

The story of the campaign has been well documented and will barely be outlined here. In 1870 activity centred on Colchester, where a by-election was being fought, the Government candidate being Sir Henry Storks (Liberal), who had administered the Contagious Diseases Acts in Malta, as Commanding Officer. The abolitionists felt they had a chance, by the promotion of a candidate, of splitting the vote and thus frustrating the Government. General Storks (somewhat unfortunately named, in view of his support of the Acts) was on record as regretting that the Acts did not extend to servicemen's wives, a logical viewpoint which did him no good at all in Colchester, where the Acts applied. After a campaign in which the abolitionists were in danger of life and limb, Storks was defeated. This success proved a turning-point. The Acts were not extended to additional districts, as had been proposed.

The Royal Commission upon the Administration of the Contagious Diseases Acts, which has already been referred to, was set up because of the widespread concern which followed full public realization of existence of the legislation. The only conclusion it seems safe to draw from the evidence given to the Commissioners is that the Acts 'brushed the crumbs under the carpet' and cleaned up the streets as, in our own time, has the Street Offences Act, 1959, promoted by Josephine Butler's great-nephew by marriage, the present Lord Butler. Castle Street, Plymouth, formerly notorious as 'Castle Rag', became relatively respectable and there was a lessening of disorderly conduct in the streets, though the increased vigilance of the police and the closing down of beerhouses may also have contributed to this. The unproved and much-disputed claim made by defenders of the Acts that they had affected a reduction in the number of prostitutes rather lost its force when other defenders of the Acts took the standpoint of Mr R. T. Pickthorn, visiting surgeon to the Devonport district, who informed the Royal Commission: 'My private opinion is that the number [of prostitutes] could be too much reduced, considering the morals of the men who reside in this district' (C. 408–1, Qn. 1624).

In 1871 the Royal Commission produced a report, which was not implemented, recommending a reversion to the position laid down by the 1864 Act, whereby those prostitutes only who were suspected of being diseased were subject to regulation. The chief claim to fame of this Commission is not their recommendations, but their enunciation of the current double standard of morality:

> We may at once dispose of this recommendation [that soldiers and sailors should be subject to regular examination], so far as it is founded on the principle of putting both parties to the sin of fornication on the same footing by the obvious but not less conclusive reply that there is no comparison to be made between prostitutes and the men who consort with them. With the one sex the offence is committed as a matter of gain; with the other it is an irregular indulgence of a natural impulse (C. 408, para 60).

At a time when much prostitution was thought to be an alternative to sheer destitution, this was too much even for some of the Commissioners' Victorian contemporaries.

Professor J. H. Plumb has described the London of the mid-nineteenth century as 'Nearer to Port Said between the wars than to the London of today.' He continues:

> Anyone could buy a virgin of 12 for a few shillings. The upper-class Victorian male did not treat servants or working-class girls as

he treated women of his own class. They were fair game, and if the servant got into trouble, it was her fault and she was sent packing. In the slums, hunger drove thousands on to the streets. Asked why she traded herself, one small girl replied 'for meat pies'. It was not surprising perhaps that one Victorian gentleman's 'bag' ran into hundreds.[3]

The essentials of this situation were reproduced in the garrison and sea-port towns, with a modification of scale and of the type of 'customer'; it must be remembered that many of the servicemen involved were no more than boys, as much in need of help and guidance as the prostitutes themselves. Josephine Butler discovered this on visiting brothels: she was shocked at the youth of the lads, who told her they visited the brothels because everyone else did and because they had nowhere else to go.

The most valuable recommendation of the Royal Commission of 1871 was the raising of the age of consent from 12 to 14. 'The traffic in children for infamous purposes is notoriously considerable in London and other large towns. We think a child of 12 can hardly be deemed capable of giving consent, and should not have the power of yielding up her person' (para. 59). In 1875 the age of consent was raised to 13.

Josephine Butler's attitude is revealed in the answers she gave to the Commissioners investigating the Contagious Diseases Acts, who asked her to give evidence on short notice. Most of the questions and answers naturally related to the main theme, that is, the effect of the regulation of prostitution, but Mrs Butler also found occasion to remark:

A girl who has no education has a vacant mind, ready to be engaged with trifles. (Qn. 12,885)

Well, if you only give us equal laws we will not complain. Let your laws be put in force, but let them be for male as well as female, and let them include civilian gentlemen. (Qn. 12,939)

So long as men are vicious and women have no employment this evil [prostitution] will go on. (Qn. 13,033)

In my own industrial home I have had sewing and envelope making, and work from shops, and different kinds of industrial occupation for them. (Qn. 13,114)

To Mrs Butler, the connection between destitution and prostitution seemed obvious; destitution was the result of lack of employment for women and the starvation wages paid to seamstresses and other women workers; these evils, in their turn, were related to the absence of educational and training facilities for girls, so that women workers comprised mainly unskilled and low-grade labour. The blame for this sad state of affairs, she considered, lay on a male-dominated society which denied women the parliamentary vote and allowed them little influence on public affairs. She was not so naïve as to think that poverty was the only cause of prostitution but saw it – and rightly, in the conditions of the times – as a major factor.

The gap between the conventional, male attitude of the Commissioners and Mrs Butler's viewpoint is shown in an interchange on the suggested extension of the Acts to towns other than the sea-port and garrison towns where they were in operation.

> You would not recommend the extension of these Acts to the civil community?
> I do not understand that question, because they now apply only to the civil community. (Qn. 12,897)
> The Acts operate only in certain specified districts?
> I am perfectly aware of that. (Qn. 12,898)
> And one question which has been referred to this Commission is whether it is desirable to extend these Acts to the whole country?
> I perfectly understand that, but those who are dealt with are women – not soldiers and sailors, but civilians. (Qn. 12,899)
> They apply to a certain class?
> But they are civilians, are they not? What is the meaning of the question 'Shall we extend them to civilians?' (Qn. 12,900)
> To all the prostitutes in the country.
> That is putting it plainly. Now I understand. (Qn. 12,901)

Mrs Butler was undoubtedly in the right; the Acts were *for the benefit* of soldiers and sailors but applied to civilian women only.

Mrs Butler also gave evidence to the Select Committee on the Contagious Diseases Acts, the reports of which were published between 1879 and 1882.[4] By that time she could claim thirty years' experience, having 'helped fallen women since 1851'. Her attitude was that the Acts were liable to turn a woman within their scope into 'a vessel periodically cleansed for public use'. She commented that: 'A woman on the register, if she seeks and obtains a situation, is liable to have a policeman constantly looking her up' (Qn. 5352). Her sympathies extended to the young soldiers at the brothels she had visited. She commented:

> There were boys there who appeared to me to be not more than 13 years of age, very boyish; some may have been 17, 18 or 20, but they were extremely youthful in appearance. Some of them had just joined; some of them had a look of perfect innocence, like boys brought from the country.   (Qn. 5368)

She claimed to 'study the matter with a view to reclaiming women ... and with a view to reclaiming men quite as much' (Qn. 5375), adding, 'It appears to me a simple want of common sense to apply a law to one sex only' (Qn. 5377).

Had Mrs Butler not been called to lead the campaign against the Contagious Diseases Acts, she would undoubtedly have pursued her earlier feminist interests, particularly education (she was President of the North of England Council for Promoting the Higher Education of Women). Many regretted her withdrawal from these activities. She was particularly well placed to help in the field of women's education, her husband being Principal of Liverpool College and a noted educationist.

To a modern mind, one of the most astounding aspects of Mrs Butler's attitude was her indifference to the efforts made to check venereal disease. While she wished for all infected persons to receive hospital treatment on a voluntary basis, she was obviously uninterested in this aspect of the matter, holding that whereas it might be impossible to avoid contracting some types of infectious disease, no one need put himself in the position where venereal disease was contracted. Her comments to the Commissioners include: 'Recollect, however, that they [infected persons] cannot spread this disease except through the wilful concurrence of the person infected in a sinful act' (Qn. 12,934). 'Men and women can avoid that disease by voluntary self-control, and I think it is a mischief to meddle with it at all' (Qn. 12,941). Her attitude did not change much in the decade between the Royal Commission and the Select Committee, as the following interchanges with the Committee members show:

> Is it not a fact that the first consideration put before the world in these Acts is health?
> Certainly. (Qn. 5433)
> And you would prefer before that the moral and constitutional questions involved in such laws?
> Certainly, the moral principle involved in it is enough, because health will follow upon morality, and only upon morality.
> (Qn. 5434)

Mrs Butler was against vice, rather than disease.

In opposing the Acts, Josephine Butler faced a problem which we still face today – the difficulty that the police, while conscientious in the performance of thankless tasks, are not infallible, and enquiries into allegations against officials are made by other officials, so that, even if justice is done, it is not seen to be done. A dangerous feature of the Acts was that women could be apprehended as prostitutes on police suspicion. The doctrine of police infallibility was supported both by the Royal Commission of 1871 and the Select Committee of 1879–1881, in spite of the fact that in the intervening period a woman, Mrs Percy, who was not a prostitute, had been driven to commit suicide through harassment under the Acts. John Stuart Mill, on giving evidence to the Royal Commission in 1871, emphasized that the police had to have considerable discretion if they were to make the Acts effective, and that such discretion was a distinct danger to the liberty not only of prostitutes, but incidentally and unintentionally, of all women (Qns. 19,990–4). The Select Committee would have none of this, reporting: 'Your Committee are not satisfied that in a single case the action of the police has been marked by the carelessness and misconduct somewhat recklessly attributed to them' (p. xxii). It concurred with the Royal Commission: 'That the police are not chargeable with any abuse of their authority and that they have hitherto discharged a novel and difficult task with moderation and caution' (p. xxii).

A tragic sidelight is thrown on the condition of some of the prostitutes living in the environs of sea-ports and garrison towns by the Select Committee's claim:

> Before the passing of the Acts women of this class [prostitutes] were sunk in a state of disease and misery which baffles description. They are represented as living 'like wild beasts' in woods and drains, without shelter, and almost without clothing, and without the slightest regard to, or conception of, ordinary decency (p. xxvi).

The truth of the matter seems to be that any sort of supervision by police, medical authorities or charitable workers, however much disliked by the recipients, was, from a physical point of view, better than the sheer neglect previously accorded to these women for whom the economy had no place. The claim by members of the Select Committee that the Acts led to an improvement in the physical condition of the women involved was to some extent justified.

While many of the prostitutes bitterly resented the physical examinations to which they were subjected, others treated the certificate they obtained as a 'licence to trade'; they were more or less 'Queen's women'. Both results were obnoxious from the point of view of Josephine Butler and the abolitionists.

The campaign by the abolitionists released scurrilous abuse on those involved, but nevertheless had its effect and in 1879 Parliament, still unable to make up its mind, appointed the Select Committee referred to above. A powerful champion of abolition had arisen in the House of Commons, James Stansfeld, who forewent his chance of office through support of the cause. The Select Committee recommended the retention of the Acts but, as has been the case not infrequently, a minority report, in this instance drawn up by Stansfeld, was more influential than the majority recommendations. Stansfeld advocated abolition and in 1883 promoted a motion condemning compulsory medical examinations; this was carried and the Acts were suspended, to be repealed three years later.

The success of the campaign led to a certain change in direction rather than a lessening of Josephine Butler's activities. The 'regulation of vice' had been stopped in this country but the vice continued and the white slave traffic flourished. Regulation of prostitution persisted overseas and Josephine Butler became a dominant figure in a worldwide organization for the suppression of the state regulation of vice; she continued her rescue work for 'fallen women' at home, and did not give up until 1901. The Josephine Butler Society, which succeeded The Association for Moral and Social Hygiene, is still active today and is the British branch of the International Abolitionist Federation, founded by Mrs Butler in 1875. In all accounts of the women's emancipation movement, Josephine Butler is honoured as a heroine. Her contemporary feminists, however, were far from united in supporting her in the heat of the struggle, mostly from ultra-respectability and the fear of harming other feminist causes; as already mentioned, the women's suffrage movement split in 1871 on account of Mrs Butler's campaign.[5] It is also interesting to note that Dr Elizabeth Garrett Anderson supported majority medical opinion on the desirability of the Contagious Diseases Acts.

Josephine Butler's attitude of mind was not (somewhat naturally) one which would be universally accepted today. Like Gladstone, who was also interested in 'fallen women', she viewed life in terms of religion and her relative lack of interest in public health has been mentioned. Nevertheless, Mrs Grundy was no longer able to obscure the facts of life after Josephine Butler's campaign. At a time when hospitals had to depend on voluntary donations, there was very little provision for the treatment of venereal diseases outside the armed forces, for the respectable and charitable wished to help the deserving poor, rather than the undeserving, but Josephine Butler's recommendation for increased treatment facilities on a voluntary basis was the policy eventually adopted in this country. Her pamphlet, *The Constitution Violated* (1871), was a spirited claim for the constitutional rights of a despised sector of the community; she agreed with Jacob Bright that the Contagious Diseases Acts were examples of class legislation, aimed at the poorer class of women; anyone who could afford to ride about in a carriage was necessarily exempt from the attentions of the police. As well as being an example of class legislation, the Contagious Diseases Acts were blatant examples of sex discrimination and the campaign against them rightly has a place in the records of the movement for the emancipation of women.

Mrs Butler's personal morals were above suspicion; she was happily married and a devoted mother, describing herself to the Select Committee of 1879 as 'a mother of sons'. Her only daughter sustained a tragic, accidental death in early childhood and provided the motivation to 'go forth and find some pain keener than my own, to meet some people more unhappy than myself'. Although she could, with pain and compassion, contemplate vice, her personal modesty was to the modern mind so excessive that she preferred to go through her confinements without the aid of a qualified physician rather than submit to male medical examination. A letter she wrote to a friend, when in ill-health, throws light upon her outlook. In this letter of February 22nd, 1868, she refers to the pioneer woman doctor, Elizabeth Garrett, later to become Elizabeth Garrett Anderson:

> But for Miss Garrett . . . I gained more from her than from any other doctor . . . *because* I was able to *tell* her so much more than I ever could or would tell to any *man*. . . . Is it desirable that the finest most sensitive part of a woman – that which God gave her, should on the one hand be wounded with such a wound as no proud and gentle nature ever recovers from, or else should on the other hand be deadened so that the woman becomes only half herself, and this is what the tyranny of the medical profession has accomplished?
> O it is shame, shame! and not a few of us *choose to die* rather than be guilty of what we feel before God is unbearable and *not the will of God that we should bear*. I pray God that other Miss Garretts may arise. . . . Men cannot conceive of the exquisite purity of young girls. . . . My beloved mother had 12 children and never had a doctor near her. I followed her example and was carried safely thro' every confinement . . . we trust in God, and if we die we do so willingly in a protest against wicked customs.[6]

One cannot help wondering how women reared to such an exquisite state of sensibility and modesty could bear to marry at all and, indeed, as Queen Victoria indicated on various occasions, they were wont to find the married state somewhat of a shock. To quote Elizabeth Longford:

> In some moods she [Queen Victoria] found herself doubting whether it was ever the right moment to bear a child 'for it is such a complete violence to all one's feelings of propriety (which God knows receive a shock enough in marriage alone)'.[7]

A certain dislike of natural processes seems to have been common amongst well-bred Victorian women. One must remember, however, that in coarser ages than the Victorian it was thought unseemly for physicians to supervise births except by remote control; also, Mrs Butler attributed a similar sensitivity to men, considering that they would not care to be examined by a female physician.

The tone of Josephine Butler's public utterances tends to be so fervent and pious that one is surprised to learn (from Mlle Amélie Humbert) that she was 'very humourous'. On one occasion Mrs Butler was stranded at Neuchâtel railway station and helped by two voluntary agents of the International Union of the Friends of Young Women. When at last she arrived at Mlle Humbert's house she declared, 'I have been rescued! I was a poor, lost, shipwrecked woman, and the young women of your Association have saved me!'[8]

The student of the Victorian scene cannot help but be amazed by the contrasts it presents; the extreme religiosity and prudery of the dominant middle-classes on the one hand and the coarse life of the labouring-classes, particularly in the towns, on the other. The life of the masses, with its endemic addiction to drink, the swarms of prostitutes and the extensive criminal activity is in such marked contrast to the ignorance which was thought fitting for the well-brought-up young woman. The very success of the Victorian middle-class woman in adapting (or distorting) herself to the favoured sexual type of the period was a reason for men resorting to prostitutes; after the 'Angel in the House', one can understand the desire for something more earthy.

The feminist movement, as has been indicated, was essentially middle-class and that section of it associated with Josephine Butler was charitable rather than emancipated. It supported the prevailing moral code, fighting the hypocrisy which preferred to assume that what was supposed to happen did, in fact, happen. One can see some of the influences at work during the period which affected moral attitudes. To begin with, the country was suffering from one of its cyclical attacks of puritanism, partly as the result of religious revival, partly due to royal influence and partly to the dominance of the middle-classes. On the whole, the wealthy classes provided for their women financially, whether chaste or unchaste. A legitimate heir had to be provided but, with this duty behind her, the aristocratic woman would not expect to starve if she strayed from the path of virtue. The economic argument applied also to many working-class women. If they had to rely on their own efforts for subsistence, then loyalty to their husbands was not a matter of economic necessity. Often the husband was not around, as is the case in New York Negro society and elsewhere today. To the middle-class woman, virtue was a matter of necessity, though she was not making a virtue of necessity so much as accepting a code of behaviour to which she had been conditioned and which put her in a position of superiority to the class beneath her; the middle-class woman's superiority depended upon the combination of her respectability and relative wealth. The feminists combined altruism with their respectability and would, one feels, have worked for social welfare in any age where this had been possible. Josephine Butler's campaign was unique within the feminist movement in that it tried to help women drawn from a working-class rather than a middle-class background.

Notes

1 Report of Select Committee of the House of Lords on the Contagious Diseases Acts, 1866. Session 1867–8 (113).

2 Parl. Deb., 3 S, Vol. 203, cc. 508–1.

3 *The Sunday Times*, 30.11.1966, 37 (colour supplement). Article: The Class War: 2. When Men and Women knew their Place. (The 'Victorian gentleman' is presumably Walter of *My Secret Life*.)

4 Report from the Select Committee on the Contagious Diseases Acts, together with the proceedings of the Committee, Minutes of Evidence and Appendix. C. 323, July 30th, 1879; C. 114, March 10th, 1880; C. 308, Sess. 2, July 26th, 1880; C. 351, July 28th, 1881 (Vol. I); C. 340, August 7th, 1882 (Vol. II).

5 Rover, Constance, *Women's Suffrage and Party Politics in Britain, 1866–1914*, 1967.

6 The letter quoted is taken from the Fawcett Library collection and is amongst copies of letters from Mrs Butler given to E. M. Turner by Dame Millicent Fawcett in 1928. The 'Dear Friend' appears to be Albert Rutson. It will be recalled that E. M. Turner and Dame Millicent jointly acted as biographers for Josephine Butler. Un-

fortunately, this group of letters is in the form of typed copies, not original manuscript.

7 Longford, Elizabeth, *Victoria R.I.*, 1964, 338.

8 Humbert, Amélie, *The Spiritual Side of the Life-Work of Josephine E. Butler*, 1908, 10. Originally an address delivered to the 34th Annual Meeting of the Friends' Abolitionist Association.

10

White Slavery

W. T. Stead: 'It can't be true, it would raise Hell.'
Benjamin Scott: 'It doesn't even rouse the neighbours.'

It is possible for people of goodwill to differ from Mrs Butler in her attitude to the Contagious Diseases Acts and to consider her campaign misguided; it is scarcely possible, however, to do other than admire her efforts to stop the traffic in young girls, for immoral purposes, between England and the Continent, and to have the age of consent raised. In these campaigns, the honours are shared between Mrs Butler, the Salvation Army, the journalist and editor W. T. Stead, and Benjamin Scott, Chamberlain of the City of London.

In the course of her investigations, Mrs Butler had come to realize that young girls were being shipped from London to Brussels where they were kept in brothels, contrary to Belgian law, which did not permit the inmates of brothels to be minors, unless placed there with their parents' consent. To quote from her *Personal Reminiscences of a Great Crusade:*

> On the 1st May, 1880, I published in England a statement which was afterwards reproduced in French, Belgian and Italian journals, in which occurred the following words:–
> 'In certain of the infamous houses in Brussels there are immured little children, English girls of from ten to fourteen years of age, who have been stolen, kidnapped, betrayed, carried off from English country villages by every artifice, and sold to these human shambles.

The presence of these children is unknown to the ordinary visitors; it is secretly known only to the wealthy men who are able to pay large sums of money for the sacrifice of these innocents.' There followed a recital of incidents which had been sworn to by witnesses, but which I need not repeat. I concluded with the words: 'A malediction rests on those cities where such crimes are known and not avenged.' [1]

M. Levy, *Juge d'Instruction* of Brussels, challenged Mrs Butler to produce evidence of her allegations, demanding of the Home Secretary (Sir William Harcourt) that she should make a deposition on oath under the Extradition Act. Josephine Butler's friends seem to have advised against her complying with this request but nevertheless she insisted on making the deposition, taking the sensible attitude that if she did not do so, it would be thought she could not prove her charges. A copy of this deposition, which was printed and supplied to the Association for Moral and Social Hygiene for private circulation only, may be seen at the Fawcett Library, London. Her deposition was unchallenged, as her evidence was irrefutable and further supporting evidence came to light. Although the revelations led to a certain clean-up in Brussels, it did not put an end to the white slave traffic.

It is interesting to find that in the year of Mrs Butler's public disclosures, 1880, debates took place in the House of Commons on an Assault on Young Persons Bill (Bill 304), a private members' measure, and two M.P.s spoke in favour of a reduction of the age of 13, which was cited in the Bill. The background to the measure was disquiet concerning a case of indecent assault on a little girl of six, where no conviction could be obtained because the prisoner pleaded consent. The member for Stockport (C. H. Hopwood) brought in a Bill to cope with the situation and the Home Secretary (Sir William Harcourt) promised to do all he could to facilitate it. However, Mr G. W. Hastings (Worcestershire) informed the House:

An alteration was necessary with regard to the second clause which fixed the age of 13 as the lowest age. . . . He proposed to reduce the age specified in the Clause to 10 years. . . . He was convinced the limit of the age in the Bill was fixed far too high, and that the age of 10 would be quite as high as it ought to be.[2]

He proceeded to move an amendment to this effect, which was supported by Mr C. N. Warton (Bridport), who stated:

> He regarded the age of 13 as much too high, and was in favour even of a lower age than that named in the amendment of the Honourable Member for East Worcestershire. The Solicitor General probably knew that 12 was the legal age of marriage.[3]

In mitigation of the members' attitude it should be mentioned that 'indecent assault' covered actions of much lesser gravity than rape, but it is to the credit of the House that the amendment was lost.

Another result of Josephine Butler's revelations was the formation by the City of London of the Association for the Suppression of the Traffic in Women and Girls. This Association was formed largely at the instigation of Benjamin Scott, who was secretary of the City of London Committee for the Repeal of the Contagious Diseases Acts. He and Mrs Butler hoped to push Parliament into taking action to control the traffic in girls and as the result of their pressure a Select Committee of the House of Lords was set up in 1881, which reported in 1882[4] confirming the charges made. The Committee 'appointed to inquire into the state of the Law relative to the PROTECTION OF YOUNG GIRLS from Artifices to induce them to lead a Corrupt Life, and into the means of Amending the same' found that girls had been induced to go to Belgium and elsewhere for immoral purposes and that although the girls were not, in the main, of good character and in most instances knew they were going abroad for immoral purposes, they did not know that they would be practically prisoners. The girls were 'in debt to the keepers for whose benefit they were employed, and their own clothes taken from them' (I–4); also, 'In many instances these girls were under 21, and the Belgian law on this point was evaded by the production of false certificates of birth procured by the *placeurs* from Somerset House . . . (I–5). Their Lordships went on to criticize English law: 'In other countries female chastity is more or less protected by law up to the age of 21. No such protection is given in England to girls above the age of 13' (II–8).

No doubt the contrast their Lordships had particularly in mind was that of Belgian law, which made it an offence to seduce a girl under 21 years of age for the purpose of prostitution, unless the

5 A seventeenth-century male obstetrician operating under a sheet. This is illustrative of the prudery which used to surround childbirth *Wellcome Historical Medical Library*

6a   Josephine Butler

6b   A meeting, during the womens campaign against the
Contagious Diseases Acts   *By permission of the Salvation
Army Literary Department and Lt.-Col. Madge Unsworth, in
whose book, 'Maiden Tribute', these illustrations were reproduced*

girl had been placed in a brothel by her parents, in accordance with police regulations. The penalty for contravention of the law was imprisonment for a period which could vary from three months to two years.

The Committee members also criticized English Society: 'The evidence before the Committee proves beyond doubt that juvenile prostitution, from an almost incredibly early age, is increasing to an appalling extent in England, and especially in London' (II–9).

Like many worthy people before and since, they endeavoured to find a reason for this sorry state of affairs, stating:

> Various causes are assigned for this: a vicious demand for young girls; overcrowding in dwellings, and immorality arising therefrom; want of parental control, and in many cases a parental example, profligacy, and immoral treatment; residence, in some cases, in brothels; the example and encouragement of other girls slightly older, and the sight of the dress and money, which their immoral habits have enabled them to obtain; the state of the streets in which little girls are allowed to run about, and become accustomed to the sight of open profligacy; and sometimes the contamination with vicious girls in schools (II–10).

From the evidence given to the Committee one gathers that while many of the girls abducted were not 'of good character', nevertheless they were not, in the main, hardened prostitutes, for it was very important to the *placeurs* that the girls should not be diseased; also there appears to have been a number of cases where the girls were genuinely deceived as to the nature of the work (usually described as that of 'barmaid') which they would be expected to undertake.

Their Lordships recommended changes in the law so as to clamp down on the *placeurs*, tighten up Somerset House procedure regarding birth certificates and to raise the age of consent to 16; they also recommended that the age of unlawful abduction for immoral purposes should be raised from 16 to 21. A Bill based on the House of Lords' report was introduced in that House in 1883, 1884 and 1885 and passed through but, on the two former occasions, it was lost in the House of Commons. A similar fate seemed to be awaiting the Bill in 1885 and would, no doubt, have ensued, had not Benjamin Scott, after consulting Josephine Butler, approached the journalist W. T. Stead. Stead at first refused to believe the evidence and then decided to test it. He proved that he could buy a child, keep her in a brothel overnight and send her to Paris the next day by actually doing so with a girl, Eliza Armstrong, whom he bought from her mother for £5. The child was looked after carefully in a private room of the brothel and taken to Paris by a woman who was a member of the Salvation Army, but who could have been anybody. Stead publicized the knowledge of the traffic in girls which he had obtained in the *Pall Mall Gazette*, of which he was editor. His tactics did credit to his journalistic flair. On Saturday July 4th, he announced that the Criminal Law Amendment Bill was for the third time threatened with extinction by the House of Commons and that he was therefore proposing to publish the report of his 'Special and Secret Commission of Enquiry'. He added:

> Therefore we say quite frankly today that all those who are squeamish, and all those who are prudish, all those who prefer to live in a fool's paradise of imaginary innocence and purity, selfishly oblivious of the horrible realities which torment those whose lives are passed in the London Inferno, *will do well not to read the Pall Mall Gazette of Monday and the three following days*. The story of an actual pilgrimage into hell is not pleasant reading.[5]

The following Monday (July 6th) the first article under the heading of *The Maiden Tribute of Modern Babylon* appeared. He stated, 'I do not ask for any police interference with the liberty of vice. I only ask for the repression of crime.'[6] The crimes he had in mind were:

(1) The sale and purchase and violation of children
(2) The procuration of virgins
(3) The entrapping and ruin of women
(4) The international slave trade in girls
(5) Atrocities, brutalities and unnatural crimes.

Horrific examples are given. Under Item 2 he wrote:

> Some are simply snared, trapped and outraged either when under the influence of drugs or after a prolonged struggle in a locked room, in which the weaker succumbs to sheer downright force. Others are regularly procured; bought at so much per head in some cases, or enticed under various promises into the fatal chamber. . . .[7]

An 'experienced officer', who seems to have been Benjamin Scott, an honest but hardly unbiassed witness, was cited as saying: 'Of course they are rarely willing and as a rule they do not know what they are coming for.'[8]

In answer to Stead's question, 'But do the girls cry out?', the 'experienced officer' said, 'Of course they do. But what avails screaming in a quiet bedroom?'[9] Much more sensational material followed, under headings such as:

The confessions of a Brothel Keeper
The London Slave Market
How Girls are Bought and Ruined
Buying Girls at the East End
A Girl Escapes after being Sold
A Dreadful Profession (the certification of children as virgins before molestation)
Why the Cries of Victims are not Heard (underground rooms).

Stead went on to criticize the law, which he considered gave aid to the criminal:

If a child of 14 is cajoled or frightened . . . into unwilling acquiescence . . . the law steps in to shield her violator. If permission is given, says *Stephen's Digest of the Criminal Law*, the fact that it was obtained by fraud, or that the woman did not understand the nature of the act, is immaterial.[10]

On the following day, July 7th, Stead described the procuring of nurses and shop girls. His informant told him:

Young girls from the country, fresh and rosy, are soon picked up in the shops as they run errands. But nurse girls are the great field . . . there are any number in Hyde Park every morning, and all virgins.[11]

The trade was well organized and reproductions are given of certificates used to protect the client from fraud or legal consequences. Examples given include the following: W

June 29, 1885
This is to certify that I have examined —— W——, aged 17 years and —— K——, aged 17 years, and have found them both virgins.
———— M.D.

AGREEMENT

I hereby agree to let you have me for £......, and will come to any address you send me at two days' notice.

Name ....X.................... (her mark) Aged 17
Address   318 S.................................... St.[12]

The articles were continued throughout the week until Friday, July 10th, all under the *Maiden Tribute* heading except that of July 9th, which gave 'The Truth about our Secret Commission'. Stead described juvenile prostitution, the entrapping of Irish girls and much more of the seamy side of London life, claiming that the law facilitated abduction. Perhaps the most telling of his disclosures was his account on July 7th of the purchase of a child of 13 for £5. Some of his final disclosures related to the foreign export trade and he supplemented the series by a discussion of the Criminal Law Amendment Bill. The scandal evoked was such that the Bill in question received its second reading on the evening of July 9th and became law on August 14th, 1885, though not without some opposition.

An amusing sidelight thrown up by the debates was that the police, alleged to be so infallible in the administration of the Contagious Diseases Acts, suddenly became both human and fallible. The member for Stoke-on-Trent, Mr H. Broadhurst, told the House:

> In the course of his walks he met many persons of the lower orders and with all honesty and sincerity he believed that if this clause (Cl. 9) were enacted it would make it absolutely dangerous for him to walk home at 1 or 2 in the morning. However efficient and impartial the police, as a rule, might be in the discharge of their ordinary duties, they were not exactly the body to be entrusted with such extraordinary powers as were given them in this Bill. They were . . . placing in the hands of the ordinary policeman the future character, prosperity and even happiness of any man whom he might think it proper to arrest.[13]

The impact made by the *Pall Mall Gazette* was acknowledged by Samuel Morley (Bristol), who stated: 'He could not avoid . . . referring to certain statements which had appeared in a London newspaper.'[14] He undertook to investigate the statements. Another

member, Mr J. A. Picton (Leicester Bo.), added: 'The newspaper
... showed conclusively that there were wrongs for which no
adequate remedy was provided....'[15]

It was W. T. Stead's subsequent trial at the Old Bailey and
imprisonment which turned him into a martyr as well as a hero. He
was charged in September 1885, together with Bramwell Booth of
the Salvation Army, Rebecca Jarrett, the reformed brothel-keeper
who had assisted him, and three others, with the abduction of
Eliza Armstrong. The essence of the case against Stead was that he
had taken the child, Eliza, away from her parents without obtaining
the consent of the father, Charles Armstrong. After this and some
associated charges were disposed of, Stead was sentenced to three
months' imprisonment. He appears to have had an impression,
which he communicated to the celebrated counsel, Charles Russell,
acting for Rebecca Jarrett, that Armstrong might not be the father
of Eliza, but the idea was not followed up. It was eventually established – too late – that Charles Armstrong was not Eliza's father
and that the mother's consent, which had been obtained, was all
that was legally necessary for Stead to have taken custody of the
child.[16]

The Criminal Law Amendment Act of 1885 was a great step
forward in the cause of public morality. The necessity for doing
more than raising the age of consent was shown by a clause in the
Act which provided that no proceedings could be taken against
girls leaving brothels wearing clothes which were not their own.
Brussels was not the only place where prostitutes could become
prisoners against their will and the charge of theft of clothes was
one way in which escaping girls were recaptured in London.

With the passing of this Act and the repeal, in 1886, of the
Contagious Diseases Acts, the feminist crusade for moral welfare
was no longer a focus of acute controversy in Britain; it was generally agreed that it was politically impossible to reinstate the Contagious Diseases Acts and undesirable to remove the protection
provided by the raising of the age of consent. All did not remain
quiet on the political front, however, for in the Empire of India,
provisions similar to those of the Contagious Diseases Acts were
still in force for the benefit of troops stationed there. After various
revelations and scandals, which included an investigation by

American ladies and the admission by Lord Roberts, the Com-
mander-in-Chief of the Indian Army, that he had been kept in the
dark by his subordinates, the brothels in the cantonments were
abolished, as was compulsory medical examination. Unfortunately
most of the hospitals and treatment centres were abolished also,
with the obvious result. The increase in disease led to a demand
for the reimposition of the regulations, emanating from women as
well as from men. In their distress at this development, the Ladies'
National Association undertook some really constructive thinking
about means to preserve the health of the troops. They advocated
the sex education of officers and men, the provision of recreational
facilities for the army and increased opportunities for men to be
accompanied by their wives, thus putting themselves in line with
modern thought. We are just beginning to realize (mainly in the
connection with the 'streaming' of schoolchildren) the extent to
which people fulfil the expectations of others. Soldiers and sailors
were expected to be dissolute and fulfilled the expectation.

In relatively modern times the League of Nations and subsequently the United Nations Organization have interested themselves in the suppression of the white slave traffic. In 1959 the
United Nations Department of Economic and Social Affairs
published a *Study on Traffic in Persons and Prostitution*. Commenting
on the report, Dr Fernando Henriques states:

> The emphasis made in the *Study* on the importance of the trend
> towards abolition (of state regulation) is extremely significant.
> If state regulated prostitution were abolished everywhere there
> is no question that the most lucrative markets of the trafficker
> would disappear.[17]

It would be seen from the above that both the *Study* and Dr
Henriques support Josephine Butler's contention that the state
regulation of vice, as she termed it, was a cause of prostitution.

There would appear to be a connection between feminism and
opposition to the toleration of brothels. (The same may be said, of
course, of many religious and humanitarian organizations. Also,
socialist and communist ideology is hostile towards prostitution,
looking upon it as one of the evils of capitalism.) In 1945 and 1962
respectively, tolerated houses were made illegal in France and Italy,

largely as the result of the activities of two remarkable women. In France, Mme Marthe Richard acted as a nurse during the Second World War and was horrified by the effects of venereal disease upon her patients. In the face of threats of violence, she amassed evidence regarding the methods used to recruit girls as prostitutes and the extensive commercial interests involved; her revelations were so appalling that the law was changed and brothels outlawed, in spite of the opposition of 'The Friendly Society of Brothel Keepers for France and the Colonies'. Similarly, in Italy, Senator Signorina Angelina Merlin introduced a bill in 1949 to close the country's tolerated houses and in 1962 the 'Merlin law' was passed, following growing disquiet over the Montesi affair of the 1950s and revelations concerning the white slave traffic organization of 'Lucky' Luciano, the Messina brothers and others. Feminist pressure has tended to operate against state toleration of brothels and it is not coincidental that pressure to change Italian law came after the enfranchisement of women in 1945 and through the medium of a woman Senator.

The connection between the British feminists and campaigns for moral welfare has not been entirely limited to the movement started by Josephine Butler, for the Pankhursts were to take up the issue, as will be described in a later chapter.

Notes

1 Butler, Josephine, *Personal Reminiscences of a Great Crusade*, 1898, 221.

2 Parl. Deb., 3S, Vol. 255, cc. 1083–4.

3 Parl. Deb., 3S, Vol. 255, c. 1086.

4 H.L. Parliamentary Papers 1881 (145) and 1882 (188).

5 Stead, W. T., 'The Maiden Tribute of Modern Babylon', in *Pall Mall Gazette*, 4.7.1885, xlii. 1.

6 *Ibid.*, 6.7.1885, 1.

7 *Ibid.*, 6.7.1885, 3.

8 *Ibid.*, 6.7.1885, 3.

9 *Ibid.*, 6.7.1885, 3.

10 *Ibid.*, 6.7.1885, 6.

11 *Ibid.*, 7.7.1885, 5.

12 *Ibid.*, 7.7.1885, 6.

13 Parl. Deb., 3S, Vol. 299, c. 203.

14 Parl. Deb., 3S, Vol. 299, c. 206.

15 Parl. Deb., 3S, Vol. 299, c. 210.

16 For a full account of the W. T. Stead campaign and the subsequent trial, see Stafford, Ann, *The Age of Consent*, 1964.

17 Henriques, Fernando, *Modern Sexuality*, 1968, 301.

II

The Feminists and Birth Control

There are two Mr M—lls, too, whom those that like reading
Through all that's unreadable, call very clever; –
And, whereas M—ll Senior makes war on *good* breeding,
M—ll Junior makes war on all *breeding* whatever!

Thomas Moore

The connection, limited though it is, between feminism and birth
control, throws into strong relief the contrast between the two
types of feminists. On the one hand there were those, such as
Richard Carlile, who supported both women's emancipation and
contraception as part of a syndrome of advanced, left-wing ideas,
and on the other, the main supporters of the 'women's movement',
who shied away from anything likely to reflect upon their respectability and thus, they felt, hinder them in their pursuit of reforms
such as educational opportunities, enfranchisement, married
women's property rights, entry into the professions and so on.

With hindsight, few would deny that the possibility of family
planning is essential to women's emancipation, but even so it is hard
to judge whether, in the period extending from the 1860s to the First
World War, the cause of women's freedom would have been better
or worse served if the feminists had been prepared to compromise
their respectability by refusing to pay lip service to the conventional
idea of marriage. Perhaps one ought not to say 'lip service', as so
many leading feminists were or had been happily married, in spite
of the current myth that most of them were frustrated spinsters.
There seems no doubt that the majority of the 'orthodox' feminists
of the period subscribed to the view that the place of the wife and
mother was at home and that, as Frances Power Cobbe put it:
'The great and paramount duties of a mother and wife once adopted,

every other interest sinks, by the beneficent laws of our nature, into a subordinate place in normally constituted minds.'[1]

One feels, at times, on going through the literature of the period, that this insistence that family duties were paramount was rather overdone but no doubt it was necessary to rebut the constant attacks on the feminists to the effect that any degree of emancipation would make women 'unfeminine' and cause them to neglect their traditional duties. A citizen of a South American republic once told the writer that, in making any public pronouncement in his country, it was necessary to start by praising the President; one feels that the nineteenth-century feminists felt it necessary, when making their claims, to assure their listeners or readers that they were not attacking the family.

In spite of John Stuart Mill's *Subjection of Women* concentrating largely upon the humiliating position of married women, nineteenth-century feminist objectives were mostly centred upon the single woman (spinster, widow or deserted wife), if one makes the very considerable exception of the campaign for married woman's property rights. This limitation was not, generally speaking, dictated by any wish to exclude married women but by the urgent need to help the single woman and by expediency. The disparity of the sex ratio and the near-destitution of governesses and other women lacking male support, led to a demand for education, training and work opportunities.[2] The demand for the vote 'on the same terms as it is, or may be, granted to men', necessarily meant that the claim related mainly to single women, so long as married women were caught by the doctrine of coverture or the qualification for the franchise was a property qualification. There were obvious advantages in asking for the vote on the same terms as men, if a claim for equality were being made.

The odium incurred by Josephine Butler and her supporters has already been referred to and there was a very real difficulty that anything touching sexual morality attracted so much attention that it was practically impossible for those involved to receive attention when they applied themselves to other fields of effort. In the U.S.A., Amelia Bloomer eventually dropped her efforts for a rational mode of dress, because (amongst other reasons) 'Bloomerism' made it difficult for her to press for women's emancipation in other directions.³ In England, one does not know how much weight to give to the motives behind the endeavour to provide training and employment for single rather than married woman. There was the obvious desire of feminine philanthropists to provide for those whose need was greatest, the equally obvious need, in view of average family size and the conditions of the time, for most mothers to be at home, and the prudential motive of disarming opposition by not asserting that a married woman's place was other than in the home; yet, during the latter part of the nineteenth century, the working-class woman in the industrial districts was in the factory and the better-off, middle-class woman had divested herself of direct domestic responsibilities and had become a lady.

Apparently, the difficulty of getting anything else done if one challenged the sexual *mores* of the time was realized by Dr Richard Marsden Pankhurst, who is believed to have rejected Emmeline Goulden's offer of a free union, partly because he did not wish her to be subject to disrespect and partly because of his commitment to various radical reforms.⁴

To be associated with the birth control movement was, in Victorian eyes, even worse than to be connected with the campaign against the Contagious Diseases Acts and the white slave traffic. Now that family planning is not only respectable but looked upon as positively desirable by public opinion in many parts of the world, it takes an effort of the imagination to realize the horror with which it was viewed in Victorian times. Part of the difficulty was the origin of contraceptive techniques on the one hand, in the case of the male condom, as a preventative against disease, and on the other hand, in the case of female appliances, as part of prostitutes' lore.⁵ Another part of the difficulty (which is still with us to some extent) was the belief that to interfere with a woman's natural propensity to have children was against religion. Opponents of birth control looked upon it as child murder, in much the same way as a section of the community looks upon abortion today.

Contraceptive techniques of sorts are of ancient origin but their slow journey towards respectability began in the post-Malthusian era when public-spirited persons developed a concern regarding population growth and the 'condition of the people'. Malthus's belief that the poor should limit their offspring by exercising self-restraint through the deferment of marriage scarcely seemed an adequate solution to what was felt to be a serious problem. (The writer recommends the second edition of Malthus's celebrated *Essay* as one of those unintentionally funny books which occasionally lightens the life of the student.)

In 1823, 'diabolical handbills' written by Francis Place, the radical tailor of Charing Cross, were being distributed; Richard Carlile (then in gaol) had been converted to the movement, but neither of these men, if size of family is anything to go by, practised what he preached. John Stuart Mill, aged seventeen at the time, was upset on walking through St James's Park to his work at the East India Office by the discovery of a newborn, strangled baby and also, on subsequently passing the Old Bailey, by the bodies of executed criminals, hanging by their necks. Shocked by the evidence of unwanted humanity, he distributed Place's pamphlets and was eventually caught and brought before the magistrates. Apparently strings were pulled and Mill was released, though it is not quite clear whether he had been sentenced by the Lord Mayor to fourteen days' imprisonment before release.[6] The matter was hushed up and Mill was careful not to compromise himself again on the issue. The incident was revived on Mill's death in 1873, when *The Times* published a damaging obituary notice. On reading this, Gladstone withdrew his support from a projected memorial for John Stuart Mill. One can understand why many of his contemporaries disliked Gladstone.

Mill's belief that discretion was the better part of valour seems to have been shared by the leaders of the 'women's movement', for although subsequent birth controllers were feminist, the leaders of the feminist movement were not birth controllers until after the First World War. It may well have been lack of imagination which was the chief determinant of feminist attitudes. To the young John Stuart Mill, abhorrence of infanticide was the motive behind his early incursion into the birth control arena. Subsequent feminists probably failed to realize that the emancipation of the average married woman from frequent pregnancies and the protracted care of children was an aim which could be pursued; the connection between family limitation and the emancipation of women, which seems so obvious to us, was by no means clear to the Victorians.

The climate of feminist thought was one in which women were looked upon as the victims of a double standard of morality, a situation which could, it was believed, be remedied if men were to exercise the sexual self-restraint expected of women. The practice of birth control, its opponents claimed, fostered sexual indulgence and may thus have seemed to the feminists to run counter to the objectives for which they were striving.

The early birth controllers were men of radical ideas, liable to include both feminism and birth control amongst a number of other 'advanced' causes without making either of these movements their main objective. A reform frequently associated with the birth control movement was that of freedom of the press, and here one sees the link with the atheists, for the laws relating to obscenity and blasphemy were the greatest restriction on freedom to print.

As with the feminist movement, there was an interaction between England and the U.S.A. in the spread of the birth control movement. Robert Owen's son, Robert Dale Owen, was a pioneer birth controller in the U.S.A., though this was but one aspect of a varied career. An American, Charles Knowlton, was the author of the celebrated *Fruits of Philosophy* (1832), the re-issue of which in England was the cause of the prosecution of Charles Bradlaugh and Annie Besant in 1877. The publicity aroused was such that from that time onwards, the birth control movement in England never looked back.

Notes

1 'What Shall We Do With Our Old Maids?', in *Fraser's Magazine*, November 1862. This and several other examples of feminist attitudes are cited in J. A. and Olive Banks, *Feminism and Family Planning in Victorian England*, 1964.

2 Cf. Rover, Constance, *The Punch Book of Women's Rights*, 1967, 17.

3 Cf. Gatty, Charles Neilson, *The Bloomer Girls*, 1967.

4 Cf. West, Rebecca, 'Mrs Pankhurst', in *The Post Victorians*, 1933, 483.

5 Cf. Fryer, Peter, *The Birth Controllers*, 1965. A full account of the history of the birth control movement.

6 Cf. St John Packe, Michael, *The Life of John Stuart Mill*, 1954, 56-9.

12

'Battling Annie'

'Love me lightly, love me long!'

George Bernard Shaw on his feeling for Annie Besant

The incredible Annie Besant (1847–1933) packed into her long lifetime the support of so many momentous causes that Arthur H. Nethercot has been able to produce a substantial volume on *The First Five Lives of Annie Besant* and to follow it with another, equally large and interesting volume entitled *The Last Four Lives of Annie Besant*.[1] Each of these various 'lives' entitles her to a place in history; nevertheless, she cannot be looked upon as an official heroine of the women's emancipation movement. One of the reasons for this is the very diversity of her activity: many of the causes she espoused were anathema to the leaders of the women's movement and as has been indicated, the one most closely related to the emancipation of women, the birth control or neo-Malthusian movement, was unacceptable to the leading feminists at the time of the Bradlaugh–Besant trial.

Annie Besant's first formal public speech was deliberately made in support of women's enfranchisement. It was good, stirring stuff, demolishing the conventional anti-suffragist arguments; for example:

> Political power would withdraw women from their proper sphere – i.e. the home. This allegation is a very odd one. Men are lawyers, doctors, merchants; every hour of the day is pledged. . . . Yet men vote. If occupation be a fatal disqualification, let us pass a law that only idle people shall have votes.[2]

The lecture was very successful and established her as a popular speaker, much in demand by her friends of the National Secular Society. Mrs Besant's interest in women's suffrage was subsidiary, however, to her interest in freethought and her subsequent lectures were on moral and religious (or perhaps one ought to say anti-religious) themes.

As a wife separated from her husband, following a marriage which she had felt to be an imprisonment, Annie Besant was naturally conscious of the unsatisfactory position of married women both legally and socially. She came to realize this even more acutely when her atheism was used as a reason for depriving her of the custody of her daughter. (On separation from her husband, it had been agreed that her son should stay with her husband and her daughter with her.) In 1878, the Rev Frank Besant's petition for custody of his daughter was granted by the Master of Rolls and although the Court of Appeal eventually gave access to the mother, Annie Besant found that her occasional visits upset her daughter so much that she determined not to visit either of her children until they had grown up. Eventually, both returned to her.

As a girl, Annie Wood (as Mrs Besant was then named) was very religious. It was the intensity with which she studied the Gospels that revealed discrepancies in the various accounts and caused her to doubt their authenticity. She resisted this for the time being but her unhappiness as a clergyman's wife caused her faith to falter, and after separating from her husband, she turned in the direction of theism. In 1874 she joined the National Secular Society. After hearing Charles Bradlaugh lecture, she realized that she accepted the position of the atheists. Soon after meeting Bradlaugh, she accepted employment on the secular journal, *The National Reformer*. Bradlaugh was an atheist, republican, neo-Malthusian and champion of freedom of the press; one might say that he was all that was anathema to respectable Victorian society, yet his personality and integrity were such that he eventually became a Member of Parliament and a respected figure within the Victorian scene. That he could become so is a tribute not only to Bradlaugh but also to the not inconsiderable sector of society in the late nineteenth century which was prepared to adopt liberal attitudes.

The celebrated Bradlaugh–Besant trial was primarily the result of a stand taken for freedom of the press, though a contributory factor was Charles Bradlaugh and Annie Besant's belief that Malthusian views on the desirability of family limitation should be propagated. They resented the prosecution of a Bristol bookseller and of the publisher, Charles Watts (1836–1906), who was a sub-editor of the *National Reformer*, for the circulation and publication of Knowlton's *Fruits of Philosophy*. As Knowlton's book had been circulating for over forty years, to refrain from challenging the authorities would be to acquiesce in the limitation of freedom and Bradlaugh and Mrs Besant accordingly formed the Freethought Publishing Company to force a test case by republishing the *Fruits of Philosophy*. This was necessary because Charles Watts had pleaded guilty to publishing an obscene book, an action which caused Bradlaugh to sever his connection with Watts.

A new edition of Knowlton's book was accordingly published and Charles Bradlaugh and Annie Besant were brought to trial in June 1877. Both conducted their own defence. Mrs Besant eloquently pleaded the case for family limitation as a means of relief to the working-class woman, and was ably assisted by Dr C. R. Drysdale, who gave evidence for the defendants. The verdict went against them, while exonerating them from any corrupt motives, but was reversed on appeal, on technical grounds.

Neither Bradlaugh nor Annie Besant thought highly of Knowlton's book so, following the trial, Mrs Besant produced a fresh work, *The Law of Population* (1877), which was sold for 6d in pamphlet form. She took the neo-Malthusian view that the relief of poverty necessitated the limitation of working-class families, described the contraceptive methods then available and refuted opponents' objections. Like Marie Stopes after her, she wished to help working-class women living in poverty, and felt it unjust that such women should be deprived of knowledge which could contribute to their happiness.

The feminists of the period all but ignored the furore created by the Bradlaugh–Besant trial and some of their leaders obviously did not wish to become involved. At his trial Bradlaugh wished to maintain, as a defence, that Malthusian thought on the general desirability of population control and limitation was part of current economic doctrine and wanted Professor Henry Fawcett, the econ-

7 Annie Besant 1885 *From 'The First Five Lives of Annie Besant', by Arthur Nethercot, published by Rupert Hart-Davis (by permission of Granada Publishing Co.)*

8 Margaret Sanger *by permission of 'Planned Parenthood World Population', New York*

omist and politician, and his wife Millicent, the feminist leader, to support him. This they refused to do, holding that the book Bradlaugh had published was objectionable.[3] The feminist press, represented at the time mainly by the *Englishwoman's Review* and the *Victoria Magazine*, refrained from commenting on the trial and one has to search for the occasional feminists, such as Lord and Lady Amberley, who combined support for the Malthusian League (which Bradlaugh reconstituted immediately after the trial) with advocacy of feminism.

Reasons for the feminist attitude have been canvassed in the previous chapter and may be summarized as lack of imagination as to the long-term results of birth control on women's emancipation, and timidity or prudence, for fear of damaging the various feminists' campaigns; perhaps the normal reticence of the middle-class woman of the time on sexual matters was a strong determinant; some of the feminists managed to overcome this in relation to Josephine Butler's campaign, but their motivation was inadequate, in the case of birth control, to cause them to override ingrained attitudes and enter the arena.

The practice of birth control spread silently amongst the English middle-class during the last quarter of the nineteenth century, but the 'women's movement' barely kept pace with public opinion; it did not number Annie Besant amongst its leaders and she, before long, turned to other causes.

Two further aspects of Annie Besant's life had feminist connotations: one was her attempt to take advantage of the opening of London University degrees to women, in 1878; the other was the organization of the match-girls' strike in 1888. Her early steps towards a science degree were successful. Coached by Dr Edward Aveling, a lecturer at King's College, London University, and a contributor to Bradlaugh's magazine, *The Reformer*, she passed her matriculation examination and embarked upon a science course, together with Bradlaugh's daughter, Hypatia. She was very successful in her early examinations but then encountered prejudice. In spite of having attained honours in a botany examination, her application to use the Royal Botanical Gardens in Regent's Park was refused by the curator on the grounds that his daughters used the gardens and could not be exposed to her (presumably malignant) presence. In May 1833, when she applied to University College, London, for admission to a practical botany class, she was refused, along with Bradlaugh's other daughter, Alice. Surprisingly, the Council of the 'Godless College' (which had been founded with the object of disregarding religious qualifications) supported the rejection of the two women. This rejection did not preclude Annie Besant from graduating from London University but she was unable to pass her examination in practical chemistry, failing three times. As she had already passed harder examinations in the chemistry course for science teachers at South Kensington, she concluded she was the victim of prejudice, for she had apparently been told by one of the examiners that he would never pass her, as he considered her activities immoral.[4] Although she never obtained her degree, she contributed to the fight made by contemporary women for higher education. One does not find an account of this in the annals of the women's emancipation movement, possibly because the prejudice against her on the part of the university (if, in fact, it existed) was on account of her atheism and Malthusianism, rather than because of her sex.

The match-girls' strike was part of Annie Besant's socialist period. She had followed her years of close friendship and co-operation with Charles Bradlaugh, whose beliefs were strongly radical, with a socialist period (first of the Fabian, then of the Social Democratic variety), when she was involved in the 'Bloody Sunday' demonstrations in Trafalgar Square in 1887 and campaigned for the rights of the lower-paid workers. This is when she became 'Battling Annie' and adopted working-class dress (in contrast to her former elegance). Together with W. T. Stead she formed the 'Law and Liberty League' with a journal, *The Link*, in which she campaigned for an increase in pay for the women at Bryant & May's match factory. In association with Herbert Burrows, she succeeded in bringing the girls out on strike and secured a slight improvement in wages and conditions, following which she was elected secretary of the Matchmakers' Union, which had just been formed. Although this episode may be said to have contributed to women's trade unionism, it was not feminist so much as socialist in intent.

In 1889 Annie Besant gave up all her freethinking, Malthusian and socialist connections and activities in favour of theosophy. She came under the influence of Mme Helena Petrovna Blavatsky, its founder, and devoted the rest of her life to the creed, which seemed to fulfil her deepest needs. Although withdrawing from her former activities, she by no means abandoned public life, being largely responsible for the development of theosophy on a worldwide basis and becoming a force in Indian politics, as a supporter of Home Rule.

Much of Annie Besant's life was a struggle to promote freedom and to combat injustice. In particular, during the years 1887 and 1889, when she espoused the cause of the lower-paid workers and was elected to the London School Board in Tower Hamlets, she emerged as a genuine social reformer. Why, then, is she not (outside theosophical circles) generally admired? The reason for this must surely be in her inconsistency. Charles Bradlaugh, always a loyal friend, was eventually disappointed in her. She left his circle for the socialists, passing first to the Fabians and then to the Social Democratic Federation. This could be looked upon as a natural progression but when she threw over everything for theosophy she went back on so much she had previously supported. She withdrew from the Malthusian League and refused to allow her *Law of Population* to be re-issued; she no longer believed in birth control by any means other than self-restraint and was prepared to consider her previous views mistaken. She also reneged upon her atheism, turning towards spiritualism, mysticism and occultism, believing, as her theosophy developed, that she received messages from masters in another world. How could she, one asks, when she had once had the courage, in a religious age, to denounce from public platforms the superstitious element in Christianity? Even worse was to follow, years later, in 1908 when Mrs Besant claimed that an Indian whom she had adopted as a boy was a sort of Messiah, a world teacher. The man in question, Jiddu Krishnamurti, renounced any claim to be a world teacher in 1929. The last thirty years of Annie Besant's life were devoted to theosophy and to India; she felt she had been Indian in previous incarnations and adopted Indian dress, making a contribution to Indian education as well as politics. She was not, of course, the first freethinker to develop an esoteric form of religion in the later years of life; it has been noted that Richard Carlile ended by calling himself 'the Revd Richard Carlile' and to some, such as Robert Owen, socialism was practically a religion; but

Annie Besant worked on a larger scale than most. Her conversion to theosophy was the result of a personal revelation which defied analysis.

Annie Besant came into conflict with Victorian sexual morality both in her public and private life. By supporting freethought and birth control, she laid herself open to abuse; supporters of birth control were *ipso facto* considered immoral and it was scarcely possible, in the nineteenth century, to separate religion from morality. Her private life made her vulnerable to criticism. As a wife who had deserted her husband she was, of course, suspect. At one time she and Charles Bradlaugh were obviously very attached and Bradlaugh's daughter, Hypatia, considered they would have married had they been free to do so. Bradlaugh was very straitlaced on moral matters and was himself parted from a wife addicted to drink; apparently he accepted the limitations of his position. Theodore Besterman, one of Mrs Besant's biographers and a theosophist, considered that neither of them would have wished to indulge in an intrigue.[5]

Annie Besant's life included a fair number of close friendships with men. During her socialist phase, she was associated with Edward Aveling and George Bernard Shaw. She was perhaps fortunate in losing the former to Eleanor Marx; a somewhat unsatisfactory association with Bernard Shaw, which apparently included one stage when she wanted to set up a joint household, ended by Shaw, who was otherwise entangled, disengaging himself. The young Cambridge graduate and socialist, Herbert Burrows, became Mrs Besant's devoted assistant in her trade union activities. Like most emancipated women, she could not find sufficient stimulus in a restricted feminine environment. The verdict of her various biographers is that it is unlikely that she ever took a lover, but somehow this seems rather irrelevant. She had a sufficiently active public life to make her private life unimportant, excepting in so far as the former resulted from the trials of the latter.

Like most prominent freethinkers of the time, Annie Besant had to meet the accusation that she favoured free love. Had she done so one feels that she would have campaigned for it openly; to be the first woman to campaign openly for birth control on public platforms must have taken tremendous courage, a quality in which she was never lacking. Her *Autobiography* (1893) is not as trenchant as her speeches and pamphlets and inclines one to think that she looked upon personal relations in terms of that extreme sensibility of feeling common in Victorian times, at least amongst the middle-classes.

It is doubtful whether Annie Besant, any more than her contemporaries, realized the close connection between birth control and women's emancipation. How could anyone, in Victorian times, foresee that the planned family would result in middle-aged women re-entering the labour market in their thousands? She believed that population limitation was necessary for the relief of poverty and that women should not be subjected to the pains and tribulations of unrestricted child-bearing. Her *Law of Population* gave practical help and, like all such pioneers, she received hundreds of grateful letters from women who felt that their families were already too much to cope with.

Notes

1 Nethercot, Arthur H., *The First Five Lives of Annie Besant*, 1961; and *The Last Four Lives of Annie Besant*, 1963.

2 Besant, Annie, 'The Political Status of Women', 1874, 11.

3 Strachey, Ray, *Millicent Garrett Fawcett*, 1913, 88–9; also Banks, J. A. and Olive, *Feminism and Family Planning in Victorian England*, 1964.

4 Nethercot, Arthur H., *The First Five Lives of Annie Besant*, 192–3.

5 Besterman, Theodore, *Mrs Annie Besant*, 1934, 106.

13

Morals and Marie Stopes

Marriage has many pains,
but celibacy no pleasures.

Samuel Johnson.

In Britain today, the best-known name among birth controllers is
Dr Marie Carmichael Stopes (1880–1956). Her *Married Love*
(1918) and *Wise Parenthood* (1918) were best-sellers and she set
up the first birth control clinic in the British Empire, as it then was.
She was unqualified medically, the title of 'doctor' relating to her
qualifications in the natural sciences. Intellectually gifted, she had
obtained a B.Sc. degree from London University, with honours in
botany and geology, before going to Munich in 1903, where she
obtained a Ph.D. On her return, she became a lecturer at Manchester
University and the research she undertook was so valuable that she
was awarded a grant by the Royal Society for research in Japan.
Had she not attained notoriety on account of her birth control
activities, she could still have been included in the annals of the
feminists as a remarkable woman who had undertaken valuable research in palaeontology, botany and zoology and who had obtained
international recognition for her research into the constitution of
coal. Much pettiness was shown at the time of her libel action against
Dr Sutherland, who had referred to her as 'a Doctor of German
Philosophy (Munich)'. Dr Stopes's qualifications included (in
addition to her Munich Ph.D.) that of Doctor of Science of London
University; she was also a Fellow of the University College of
London, a Fellow of the Zoological Society, a Fellow of the Royal
Society of Literature of London and a Fellow of the Royal Linnaean

Society of London. On occasion, opposing Counsel referred to her as 'Mrs Stopes' and 'Mrs Roe' (she was the wife of H. V. Roe of the AVRO aircraft connection). *The Times*, which had consistently refused advertisements of her books, took upon itself to alter the transcript of the lawsuit, so that the Judge's description of her as 'Dr Stopes' was altered to 'Mrs Stopes'.

In all probability Marie Stopes would not have entered the birth control area if she had not made an unfortunate marriage but (as with Annie Besant before her) this unhappy experience caused a redirection of activity. The ignorance of the Victorian middle-class young woman on sexual matters is proverbial and the contemporary mind seemed to have difficulty in distinguishing between ignorance and innocence. This is normally put down to prudery but it seems possible that other, more salacious, motives may also have been involved. Laurence Housman, in *The Unexpected Years* (1937), recounts a conversation with his stepmother:

> I remember also her defence, against my horrified protest when I discovered it, of the Victorian practice of allowing prospective brides to marry without in the least knowing what marriage meant. 'We can't afford to give it up,' she said; 'it's too attractive.' [1]

This attitude comes as somewhat of a shock but links up with what is sometimes described as the Victorian male's obsession with virginity and brothel-keepers' stratagems to meet the demand for virgins.

Annie Besant, marrying at the age of 20 in 1867, complained bitterly that her upbringing 'left me defenceless to face a rude awakening', adding 'Many an unhappy marriage dates from its very beginning, from the terrible shock to a young girl's sensitive modesty and pride, her helpless bewilderment and fear.'[2] One can easily believe Annie Besant and while one must believe Marie Stopes also, it is considerably more difficult to do so. Since Annie Besant's marriage, her own, Josephine Butler's and W. T. Stead's activities had given considerable publicity to 'the facts of life'; also, the 'gay nineties' had offset mid-Victorian prudery to some extent and the moral tone of high society had changed with the advent of the Prince of Wales (later Edward VII) as a social force. In spite of this and in the twentieth century, Marie Stopes was as ignorant as Annie Besant when, over the age of thirty, she married Dr Reginald

Ruggles Gates, a botanist whom she had met in America. After six months of marriage she felt (though did not know) that something was wrong and true to her academic habit of mind, went to the British Museum to read up the subject. As a result of her studies, she found out that her marriage had not been consummated and eventually applied to the courts (as virgo intacta) for an annulment which, on producing medical evidence, she received in 1916.

After this experience, it is not surprising that Marie Stopes felt it was high time something was done about the sex education of women. She was always prepared to act on her beliefs and published *Married Love* with a view to dispelling the ignorance of young married couples. She felt that men were ignorant also in that they did not know enough about female physiology to obtain full satisfaction for themselves and their wives, also that her book would have to be presented in a popular and simple way if it were to have any effect; she therefore tried to avoid the textbook type of presentation and to produce a book which was factually correct without blinding her readers with science. In the book there was a brief reference to contraceptive techniques which, while by no means the main theme, obviously constituted the main interest for many of of its readers; she therefore concluded that there was a need to follow up her work with another, going into this theme more fully, and published *Wise Parenthood* in the same year, in which she described methods of family limitation.

As one might expect, the books were welcomed by the Malthusian league but condemned in many other quarters; in particular her *Wise Parenthood* and subsequent setting up of a Birth Control Clinic in 1921 aroused the antagonism of the Roman Catholic Church. The reasons for opposition to publicizing contraceptive methods throws some light on current moral ideas. There was the widespread belief that contraceptive knowledge would encourage promiscuity and that fear of the consequences alone kept many girls on the straight and narrow path. This attitude was held by some medical advocates of birth control, who no doubt felt that contraceptive knowledge should be reserved for married women who chose to consult their physicians. Dr C. P. Blacker described her books as:

Obtained and read by flappers all over the country . . . these works have been responsible for providing instruction to girls of initially dubious virtue as to how to adopt the profession of more or less open prostitution. They can, in fact, in one sense, be considered as practical handbooks of prostitution, and doubtless are read by many as such.[3]

The medical profession tended to object to instruction being given in books written by a woman not medically qualified. While this point of view is understandable, obviously the sort of book Marie Stopes produced would not have been written at the time if she had not taken the plunge; many advances have been made by those who chose to ignore the restrictive practices and demarcation disputes of learning. Yet another medical objection, which applied particularly in Victorian times but was carried forward into the twentieth century, was that contraceptive practices were harmful, both physically and mentally. Perhaps this attitude derived, in part, from wishful thinking. In our lighter moments we are apt to complain that everything pleasurable is either illegal, immoral or fattening; while it used not to be quite such a sin to be fat, if one were to believe the Victorian physicians, such as Dr Acton, and some of their early twentieth-century successors, one would conclude that almost any kind of sexual activity (or even its absence) would be liable to lead to physical harm, combined with some form of dementia. This gloomy attitude, at any rate in relation to men, is implicit in the works of William Acton and other nineteenth-century medical writers. Confirmation of the state of opinion in 1894 comes from Bertrand Russell, who, at his family's instigation, had consulted the family doctor on his intention to marry without having a family.

> Birth control was viewed in those days with the sort of horror which it now inspires only in Roman Catholics. My people and the family doctor solemnly assured me that, as a result of his medical experience, he knew the use of contraceptives to be almost invariably gravely injurious to health. My people hinted that it was the use of contraceptives which had made my father epileptic. A thick atmosphere of sighs, tears, groans, and morbid horror was produced, in which it was scarcely possible to breathe.[4]

The above extract is interesting not only on account of the family doctor's attitude but also as illustrative of the probability that Lord Russell's parents used contraceptives. The division of medical opinion at the time is indicated by Lord Russell finding another doctor who assured him that contraception had no harmful effects.

There was a certain amount of objection to Marie Stopes's belief that both partners should find happiness in married love and that this required the active participation of the wife. The point of view which could not distinguish between abortion and contraception, looking on both as forms of child murder, has already been mentioned.

More firmly based were the objections, still held in some religious circles today, that contraception was against nature and that to interfere with natural processes was to flout God's injunction to man to be fruitful and multiply. Religious principles occasioned Dr Halliday Sutherland, a physician who was a Roman Catholic, to challenge Marie Stopes in a publication, *Birth Control: A Statement of Christian Doctrine against the Neo-Malthusians* (1922). In this he claimed that the poor were exposed to experiment. He stated that:

> A woman, who is a doctor of German philosophy (Munich), has opened a Birth Control Clinic, where working women are instructed in a method of contraception described by Professor McKilroy as 'the most harmful method of which I have had experience. . . .' [5]

This led to Marie Stopes bringing a libel action which was lost in the first court, won on appeal and lost again in the House of Lords. This litigation in 1923 and 1924 had much the same effect as the Bradlaugh–Besant trial of 1877 in giving the birth control movement widespread publicity.[6]

The anti-feminist view that the hazards of childbirth were necessary to keep women in their place showed itself occasionally. The very general belief that the thing to do with a tiresome woman was to give her a baby to keep her quiet may well be foreign to the young of today. Fortunately, one cannot imagine a scene such as that described by Laurence Housman in 1912, taken 'not from the slums' but 'on the borders of one of our great London Parks', occurring nowadays:

> A poor working woman, about to become a mother, was on her way home when unexpectedly her pains overtook her, and she could go no further. A policeman came to her aid, and went to find a

conveyance; and while she waited a crowd gathered, men and boys; and as they watched her they laughed and made jokes. She was a symbol to them of what sex meant; some man had given her her lesson, and now she was learning it; and to their minds it was a highly satisfactory spectacle.[7]

One criticism which could not be levied against Marie Stopes was that she was irreligious; indeed, she found herself in trouble through claiming inspiration direct from God. The fruit of this inspiration was a message she sent to the 1920 Lambeth Conference of bishops. The trouble was not the law of blasphemy but the law of obscenity. Birth control advocacy and practice was not in itself illegal in Britain, in contrast to some continental countries, but any description of sexual organs or activity in other than a strictly medical treatise was apt to be classed as obscene. In particular, a reference in *Married Love* to what we now call artificial insemination caused offence and was criticized by the Lord Chief Justice in Dr Stopes's lawsuit.[8]

The above summary of criticisms of birth control made in Marie Stopes's time and earlier had only just been written when the controversy broke out concerning the Pope's Encyclical, *Humanae Vitae*, issued in July 1968. This has been criticized so extensively by Catholics as well as non-Catholics that there is no need here to do more than refer to those sections particularly affecting the position of women. Old attitudes linger on, but at least birth control is no longer considered obscene and there is an appreciation that conjugal relations have a function in maintaining unity and harmony between husband and wife, as well as in the procreation of children. On the other hand, the Encyclical seems singularly dated in its view of birth control in relation to women and also anti-feminist (though obviously not intentionally so) in the way in which it ignores their difficulties as the sole bearers and major rearers of children. Paragraph 17 of the official English-language version of the Encyclical refers to the difficulties of men, especially the young, in observing the moral law and adds:

> It is also to be feared that the man, growing used to the employment of anti-conceptive practices, may finally lose respect for the woman and, no longer caring for her physical and psychological

equilibrium, may come to the point of considering her as a mere instrument of selfish enjoyment, and no longer as his respected and beloved companion.

Looking at contemporary Western society, one cannot but conclude that the women receiving most respect are those who have developed their personalities and talents through not being tied to the kitchen sink, day in and day out, a fate which is liable to overtake the mother of a large family. There seems little evidence that the father of a family of ten respects his wife more than the father of a family of two or, indeed, that in the case of childless couples there is necessarily any lack of respect on the part of the husband for the wife. Regarding a wife's 'physical and psychological equilibrium', one might think that this is more likely to be assisted by the absence of anxiety concerning unwanted children than by uncontrolled parenthood. The idea that a man, presumably if not constrained by the fear of adding to the number of children he must maintain, might look upon his wife as 'a mere instrument of selfish enjoyment', takes one back to the nineteenth-century attitude which inhibited some of the feminists from supporting birth control. But in those days women were not supposed to enjoy sex. To quote the Rev Kenneth Slack (Congregational Minister, City Temple, London), 'The picture of the nature of womanhood given in *Humanae Vitae* might have come from a genteel Victorian novel.'[9] This feeling that the Pope and his supporters were out of touch with the twentieth-century was not helped by the pastoral letter on the Encyclical, issued by Cardinal Heenan, Archbishop of Westminster, at the beginning of August 1968, in which he said: 'Those who have become accustomed to using methods which are unlawful may not be able all at once to resist temptation. They must not despair . . . .' This gives the impression that the use of contraceptives is looked upon as an addictive habit, pleasurable in itself and as difficult to resist as another little drink or another cigarette, from which the addict might be gradually weaned even if he could not 'all at once resist temptation'. No doubt this was not the intention, but one wonders if anyone but a celibate cleric could have phrased the matter in this way.

It is the omissions as much as the contents of the Encyclical which make one feel that it is a setback both to women and to a new view of sexual morality. Reference is made in paragraph 2 to 'A change . . . in the manner of considering the person of woman and her place in society . . .' but no appreciation is shown of the extent to which this change has resulted from family limitation. There is no specific reference to the difficulties of childbirth. As Queen Victoria so aptly put it, 'men never think; at least seldom think, what a hard task it is for us women to go through this *very often*'.[10] A Catholic mother, speaking on television on July 30th, 1968, following the Pope's pronouncement, said that she thought His Holiness could have spared a paragraph in his Encyclical for the difficulties of women and that she found difficulty in believing that a woman should have life forced out of her beyond her strength.

To revert to Marie Stopes, she was lucky that at the height of the birth control controversy she was happily married to her second husband, Humphrey Verdon Roe, who supported her in the cause and, indeed, whose money had made possible the first publication of *Married Love*. One may say she was fortunate at the crucial period, for her personal life was not without drama nor beyond criticism, though she was in no sense an immoral woman. Prior to her first, disastrous marriage, she had had a strong attachment to a Japanese scientist, Kuyiro Fujii. Eventually she became estranged from Humphrey Roe and also from her son, whose marriage she resented. She was always to enjoy male company and, like almost every advocate of advanced causes for half a century, knew Bernard Shaw, though not through any romantic involvement. Her interest in poetry and her personal efforts in that direction brought her friends amongst literary figures, including Walter de la Mare, Lord Alfred Douglas and Maurice Hewlett. In spite of her good fortune in knowing many of the interesting figures of her day and age, she suffered considerably from the enmity which her birth control activities had aroused and there were always critics ready to sneer at any activity she undertook.

The counter-arguments of the advocates of birth control are so well known and generally accepted that it is not proposed to recount them; it is, perhaps, worth mentioning, in view of the discussion of prostitution earlier in this work, that it was claimed that birth control was essentially moral, and would, in fact, check immorality, as it would enable earlier marriage without the necessity of immediately starting a family and thus discourage resort to prostitutes and other irregular arrangements.

Marie Stopes's own motives are interesting. She shared the current belief that the differential birth-rate between the classes was causing the race to deteriorate, through breeding from the unfit and the lowest stratum of society. In the climate of opinion of the time, it was difficult for members of the middle-classes not to believe that the urban poor were of inferior stock for their appearance was against them; undernourishment and unhealthy conditions took their toll; children were often barefooted and ragged and their parents work-grimed, ill-clad and unhealthy-looking. There had been an improvement since the days when Annie Besant's match-girls and later the dockers, had marched to the West End looking, to the horrified bystanders, almost like sub-human beings from another planet, but slum conditions were still deplorable. Compassion for working-class mothers was one of Dr. Stopes's strongest motives, even if she did not identify with these women. She favoured what she termed 'constructive birth control', forming the 'Society for Constructive Birth Control and Racial Progress' in 1921, but she was never able to put over the constructive side of her beliefs, exemplified by her motto 'babies in the right place'. Part of her trouble was in the name, birth control. Although contraceptive practice was obviously spreading through a large number of private decisions, public acceptance was not given to such techniques under the older term of neo-Malthusianism nor Marie Stopes's term, birth control, whether constructive or otherwise, but family planning (the term fostered by the Family Planning Association, which Marie Stopes shunned) has since gained very general public approval. What's in a name? Sometimes a very great deal, for the term, family planning, emphasized the constructive element which all the groups had at heart.

It is interesting to find that Marie Stopes's mother, Charlotte Stopes, was an active suffragist. While not at the centre of the pre-war suffrage agitation, Dr Stopes supported and to some extent participated in the struggle and was at odds with her first husband, Ruggles Gates, and her friend, Aylmer Maude (with whom she was emotionally involved) on the matter. Her biographer, Keith Briant, quotes her as writing to Maude in 1913:

My husband is beside himself with rage against 'the women' [the suffragettes] and his wife too for not condemning them. . . . You said you would not grudge me if I wanted to, or had to die for something big – bi-sexual, not like the women's cause, unisexual. What is there at present bigger than the women's movement that I could die for? [11]

In the following year (1914) she was to complain in another letter to Aylmer Maude:

I said 'We have only a few more minutes – let us have something nice to say' – and you attacked me on Tax Resistance! I wish that once at least you had come to hear me speak, then at least you could not have said what you did last night . . . perhaps I had better tell you that we 'strike no blows' – and we endeavour to make the law, making officials obey their own laws. At one sale I carried a banner in the street to the auction and a crowd of young children hooted and stoned and flung mud at us – have you ever had to wash street garbage from your hair, had the soft flesh of your neck stung with horse-dung from the road. I have. The crown of thorns was clean at any rate. . . .[12]

Marie Stopes was, of course, feminist in the wider sense of the word and, as Edith Summerskill has put it in her foreword to Muriel Box's *The Trial of Marie Stopes:*

Marie Stopes possessed in a full measure the capacity to defy those old enemies of women – custom and prejudice. Whenever we met, it was to consult on the most effective tactics of outwitting those determined to block the social emancipation of women.[13]

Her services to women were immense on at least two fronts. Her writings, in particular *Contraception: Birth Control – Its Theory, History and Practice*, published in 1923, the setting up of her clinics and the publicity attending her action for libel, gave tremendous impetus and publicity to the whole subject of family limitation and thousands of women must have obtained freedom from unrestricted childbearing as a result. Of scarcely less importance was her contribution towards killing the idea that marital relations were something suffered by the wife for the relief of the husband and her doctrine that they should provide mutual pleasure and satisfaction, a result the more easily obtainable if the fear of unwanted pregnancy were removed. Her beliefs were assisted in taking root by the idea which was seeping through from the psychologists that repression (the Victorian remedy for sexual difficulties) caused neurosis.

As an older woman, Marie Stopes was difficult to deal with and has been described by Mary Stocks as 'perhaps a little mad';[14] one is inclined to wonder whether anything worth while was ever done by anyone who could be described as 'normal'.

In the years following the First World War, the feminist organizations took up the cause of family limitation. Following the attainment of a first instalment of the vote in 1918, the National Union of Societies for Equal Citizenship took the place of the National Union of Women's Suffrage Societies, Eleanor Rathbone taking over from Dame Millicent Fawcett and support for family limitation being one of its objectives. In 1925, its Council endorsed the demand put forward by labour women and other groups that the Ministry of Health should permit public health authorities to provide birth control information for those who desired it. At last the feminists had moved to a position where, instead of barely keeping pace with public opinion, they were in the vanguard, a notable protagonist of the English birth control movement being Mary Stocks.

Although Marie Stopes's reputation overshadowed that of her British colleagues or rivals, she was not the only feminist working for family limitation. In particular, Dr Alice Vickery of the famous Drysdale family, which did so much for the Malthusian League, was associated with feminism and opened a clinic with Miss Anna Martin in south-east London where contraceptive as well as other medical advice was given. Dr Vickery was a strong supporter of the women's suffrage campaign. Edith How-Martyn and Teresa Billington-Grieg were also noted feminists who interested themselves in birth control.

There were plenty of people prepared to heap abuse on Marie Stopes and to consider her writings obscene, but it was distinctly less hazardous for feminists to support birth control in Marie Stopes's time than it was in Annie Besant's day. In 1918 the first instalment of the vote had been won and putting the clock back was not a practicable possibility, so support for family limitation could not endanger women's enfranchisement. Excepting in Roman Catholic quarters, public opinion had become more favourable towards family limitation; also, a generation of women had grown up which cared less for convention, as the suffragettes had shown and the 'gay twenties' exemplified.

The distance travelled between Marie Stopes's time and our own is shown by the Family Planning Act of 1967, empowering local authorities to supply contraceptive advice and appliances to women, regardless of marital status. The division of opinion still existing is revealed by the reluctance of many authorities to use the powers given to them, in particular in the refusal to develop domiciliary services, often the only means of reaching problem families. If ever there was a false economy from the tax- and rate-payer's point of view, it is the denial of funds for family planning services, for the maternity grants, health and welfare services related to a birth approach £200 and the family planning services work out at about £10 per annum per family served.

The difference in attitude today is also exemplified by Dr Alex Comfort's reference in *Sex in Society* to marriage manuals 'of a Stopesian squareness which is enough to make one abandon the project before the banns are up'.[15] Marie Stopes's works were thought to be the last word in outspokenness in her day!

Notes

1 Housman, Laurence, *The Unexpected Years*, 1937, 139.

2 Nethercot, A. H., *The First Five Lives of Annie Besant*, 1961, 40.

3 *Guy's Hospital Gazette*, 11.10.1924, 463.

4 Russell, Bertrand, *Autobiography*, 1967, i. 86.

5 Sutherland, Halliday, *Birth Control: A Statement of Christian Doctrine against the Neo-Malthusians*, 1922, 101–2.

6 Box, Muriel, *The Trial of Marie Stopes*, 1967.

7 Housman, Laurence, *Sex-War and Woman's Suffrage*, 1912, 50.

8 Box, *op. cit.*, 106.

9 Slack, Rev Kenneth, sermon of 4.8.1968. Quoted in the *Guardian*, 5.8.1968.

10 Letter from Queen Victoria to the King of the Belgians, 5.1.1841. See Raymond, John (ed.), *Queen Victoria's Early Letters*, 1963, 45.

11 Briant, Keith, *Marie Stopes*, 1962, 71, 73.

12 *Ibid.*, 75.

13 Box, *op. cit.*, 8.

14 *Ibid.*, 9.

15 Comfort, Alex, *Sex in Society*, 1963, 155.

14

The American Scene

Good Americans, when they die, go to Paris.

O. W. Holmes

As feminists both sides of the Atlantic had common objectives, their struggles were broadly similar but, of course, there were particular national features. Early American feminism was closely linked with the campaign for the abolition of slavery; it was also associated with the temperance movement. Feminist interest in these two movements meant an association with the Churches in the case of the more conservative sector of the women's movement, the American Woman Suffrage Association, led by Lucy Stone. The more radical National Woman Suffrage Association, led by Elizabeth Cady Stanton and Susan Anthony, favoured the reform of marriage and divorce laws, to the distress of the A.W.S.A., which supported the sanctity of traditional family life, along with their friends, the progressive clergy.

Thus the nineteenth-century American movement was split on moral issues and the Stanton–Anthony sector fell into disrepute through its support of Victoria Woodhull (see Chapter 6), who was associated with the doctrine of free love and involved in the disclosure of the scandal concerning the popular preacher, Henry Ward Beecher (brother of Harriet Beecher Stowe of *Uncle Tom's Cabin* fame). The custom of the time was for the women's suffrage associations to have male presidents and Henry Beecher was president of the American Woman Suffrage Association. Theodore Tilton fulfilled a similar function for the National Woman Suffrage

Association. When Tilton accused Beecher of adultery with his wife, it exacerbated relations between the two suffrage organizations, the former refusing to think ill of their president. The newspaper proprietor and publisher, Henry C. Bowen, in his newspaper, the *Independent*, censured the N.W.S.A. leaders, Elizabeth Stanton, Susan Anthony and Isabella Hooker, for their support of the notorious Victoria Woodhull, but 'the Woodhull' was in a position to retaliate, for Bowen was himself involved in the incredibly complex Beecher–Tilton scandal.

It is difficult to envisage what a furore this scandal created in American society but in some ways it may be compared with the subsequent Dreyfus case in France. Beecher's supporters wished to believe him innocent of adultery in face of the evidence, thus providing, in the words of his lawyers, 'safety and honour for everybody' and preserving 'the civilization and purity of American life'.[1] The social life of the time was largely centred around the church – in this case the fashionable Plymouth Church – and its popular preachers and many churchgoers felt that it was more important to uphold the ideals of the Church and the way of life it represented than to ensure that justice was done in the case of Tilton versus Beecher which came before the courts in 1875. In a similar way, in France, supporters of the verdict against Dreyfus in 1894 felt that the honour of the army and the establishment was involved and was of greater importance than a possible injustice towards a Jewish officer. The venom of the supporters of the preacher, Henry Ward Beecher, was directed against Victoria Woodhull for claiming that Beecher supported free love but had not the courage to admit it. Victoria herself did not lack this courage and became known as 'Mrs Satan'. After long-drawn-out proceedings the case against Beecher eventually resulted in a 'hung jury'.

The leaders of the National Woman Suffrage Association suffered through their support of 'the Woodhull's' feminist activities, their association with Tilton and their inability to support Henry Beecher's denials of the charges against him. All the women knew the Beechers and Tiltons, and Isabella Beecher Hooker was half-sister to Henry Ward Beecher, though apparently there was no love lost between them. Elizabeth Tilton herself cut a sorry figure throughout the affair, confessing her adultery, denying her confession and repeatedly contradicting herself. So, to some extent, did Henry Beecher, but there were many who could think no ill of their beloved preacher and resented the refusal of the suffragists to pronounce in his favour. Inevitably, the censure visited upon the leaders of the N.W.S.A. proved a setback to the women's movement as a whole.

The pressures on the nineteenth-century American male were much the same as in Victorian England. The middle-class man was not expected to marry until he was in a position to keep his wife in comfort and, when married, it was presumed that he would not make too heavy demands upon her. The idea that sex was something which a refined woman ought not to have to put up with to any extent was common to the 'respectable classes' on both sides of the Atlantic. As William Sanger put it, in his *History of Prostitution*, 'The full force of sexual desire is seldom known to a virtuous woman.'[2] In some instances, the desire to limit family size also had an inhibiting effect upon marital relations, the only generally acceptable means of family limitation being self-control.

One is normally dependent upon the writings of persons long dead for information on Victorian attitudes but fortunately these may be added to by Bertrand Russell's recent autobiography, in which he refers to his first wife, an American, whom he married in 1894, in the following terms:

> She had been brought up, as American women always were in those days, to think that sex was beastly, that all women hated it, and that men's brutal lusts were the chief obstacle to happiness in marriage. She therefore thought that intercourse should only take place when children were desired.[3]

There were, of course, large sectors of American society ignorant of or indifferent to such considerations, as well as wide regional differences. The presence and aftermath of slavery in the south deeply affected the sexual *mores* of that region and the hazards and excitement of life in the west, including gold rushes, gave to that area its peculiar character, which included phenomena such as the notorious Barbary coast. Nevertheless, the puritan ethic was not submerged and as previously indicated (see Chapter 6), the belief that the feminists stood for traditional moral standards derived from the early puritan settlers contributed to their initial successes in obtaining State suffrage.

American nineteenth-century feminists, like their English counterparts, were concerned with problems associated with prostitution. As Emily Blackwell commented, 'The higher sense of mankind says that the family is the essential unit of the state. Our practice says that the family plus prostitution is the essential unit.'[4]

There was no exact equivalent, however, to the British campaign against the Contagious Diseases Acts, for although legislation of this type was discussed from time to time, particularly when there was a scare concerning venereal disease, no such legislation was enacted. In her *Personal Reminiscences of a Great Crusade*, Josephine Butler commented upon the setting up of a New York Committee for the Prevention of the State Regulation of Vice; she also referred to efforts in St Louis to revive 'the odious system of licensing prostitution' during the period 1877–1879. In 1880 she informed the Ladies' National Association for the Repeal of the Contagious Diseases Acts of the establishment of a branch of their work in the U.S.A., to prevent the encroachment of the regulationists. She had no time for the American policy known as 'suppression of prostitution', which she described as futile, considering it regulation in a new form. The fact that men as well as women came within its scope, thus to some extent avoiding the 'double standard', did not appease her, for she held that women 'always firmly rejected such *equality of degradation*, holding in abhorrence Government assault upon the persons of either men or women'.[5] In spite of her hatred of 'vice', she considered it a mistake for laws to be passed denouncing all immorality as crime and, indeed, legislative efforts were not particularly successful. The suppression of brothels by the 'Raines Law' and consequent substitution of 'Raines Hotels' had the effect of driving the prostitutes out into the streets.

The puritan heritage in America made possible the passing of stricter moral laws than in Britain; laws varied from state to state, but in a majority of American states fornication, adultery and prostitution were (and in the latter two instances still are) penal offences. Groups of American feminists supported attempts to put down prostitution; much of the motive force behind feminism in America as well as in Britain was derived from resentment at the double moral standard which permitted men to visit prostitutes and thus bring disease into otherwise blameless families. Like their

British counterparts, women in the U.S.A. sought to raise the moral standard of American males to the exacting standard expected of middle-class women, until Freudian or neo-Freudian attitudes became an integral part of the American way of life and two world wars loosened restraints.

On the birth control front, the first prominent neo-Malthusian was British-born Robert Dale Owen (1801–1877). He was Robert Owen's eldest son, and was provoked into writing three articles, supporting birth control on sociological and economic grounds which he published in *The Free Enquirer*, a freethought journal edited by him; he also published a booklet in 1831 entitled *Moral Physiology or A Brief and Plain Treatise on the Population Question*. Owen was a feminist to the extent that he supported dress reform and, at the Indiana constitutional convention of 1850, married women's property rights. He tended to support advanced or extreme causes generally (at least, before he became a professional politician) and was a freethinker, vegetarian, teetotaller and advocate of the right of divorce. He was, of course, familiar with his father's social reforms at New Lanark and had worked in New Harmony, Indiana, where Robert Owen senior had endeavoured to found a community based on co-operation and rational education. In middle life, Robert Dale Owen had an active career as a politician, firstly in the Indiana state legislature and subsequently in Congress, and in his latter days he became a spiritualist, to the disgust of his former freethought comrades. As had been the case with Richard Carlile in England, his support of birth control and feminism was part of his general advocacy of advanced ideas and, taking his life as a whole, they did not play a predominant part. His pioneering birth control effort, however, was followed up by Charles Knowlton's influential *Fruits of Philosophy* (1832) and set in train the development which resulted in the spreading of contraceptive knowledge throughout the North-American continent, in spite of the bitter opposition of Anthony Comstock and his supporters.

The bane of the American birth controllers was the Comstock Law of 1873 (Federal Criminal Code, Section 211) that made illegal the sending of literature about contraceptives through the U.S. mails. Anthony Comstock (1844–1915) was a spiritual descendant of the witch hunters of earlier days and sought out advocates of contraception with equal ardour. He was a member of the New York Society for the Suppression of Vice and frequently worked by means of decoy letters. His activities and the law for which he was responsible had the effect of handicapping the development of medical practice, as well as resulting in the prosecution and conviction of some thousands of persons (maximum penalties were five years' imprisonment and 5,000 dollars' fine).

A genuine feminist who was to fall foul of the Comstock Laws and to become the most prominent figure in the American birth control movement was Margaret Sanger (1883–1966). Emma Goldman, who was advocating birth control simultaneously, wrote as follows:

> Neither my birth control discussion nor Margaret Sanger's efforts were pioneer work. The trail was blazed in the United States by the grand old fighter Moses Harman, his daughter Lilian, Ezra Heywood, Dr. Foote and his son, E. C. Walker, and their collaborators of a previous generation. Ida Craddock . . . paid the supreme price. Hounded by Comstock and faced with a five-year sentence, she had taken her own life. . . . The matter of priority, however, in no way lessened the value of Margaret Sanger's work. She was the only woman in America in recent years to give information to women on birth control and she had revived the subject in her publication after many years of silence.[6]

Margaret Sanger was a socialist and a supporter of women's suffrage. The origin of her interest in contraception was her work as a nurse and the insight she obtained into the lives of working women and the prevalence of abortion. Some talks and articles on health brought her into conflict with the Comstock Law, for she had been daring enough to mention the names of venereal diseases in an article, which was suppressed by the Post Office on Anthony Comstock's complaint.

In spite of a medical environment, Margaret Sanger was unable to make herself well informed about contraceptive techniques in America and accordingly went to France, where she obtained much fuller information. On her return she founded a journal, *The Woman Rebel*, which was feminist, revolutionary and in favour of birth control. This was an outright challenge to Comstockery and resulted in the journal being banned from the mails. The press was able to have a little amusement over 'Woman Rebel Barred From Mails', suggesting the 'mails' should be spelt differently. To avoid imprisonment, which she felt would inevitably result from the indictments she had to face through publication of *The Woman Rebel*, Margaret Sanger fled to England in 1914, but not before producing a comprehensive pamphlet on birth control under the title of *Family Limitation*. In England she circulated in birth control circles and met Marie Stopes at a meeting organized by Edith How-Martyn, the suffragette. In her absence from America her husband, William Sanger (an artist, not to be confused with his namesake, the author of the *History of Prostitution*) and Emma Goldman were imprisoned under the Comstock Laws. She was fortunate in finding, on her return to the U.S.A., that the charges against her had been dropped. However, she was subsequently sentenced and imprisoned for opening a birth control clinic in Brooklyn in 1916. In 1917 Margaret Sanger's journal, *Birth Control Review*, was first issued and in 1921 she became president of the American Birth Control League. Like Marie Stopes in England, she had to meet the opposition of the Roman Catholic Church.

One feels that Margaret Sanger, a tomb-cutter's daughter and one of eleven children, was closer to the working women whom the birth control campaign was designed to help than was Marie Stopes, but after marrying a wealthy oil magnate in 1922 there was a certain change of attitude, resulting in an alliance between Margaret Sanger and the progressive element in the medical profession and favouring medical control of contraceptive knowledge, rather than its direct dissemination to all who wished to have it. Although this change of stance was looked upon by many as regressive, the alliance with a sector of the medical profession may well have helped to sap the strength of Comstockery. The Comstock Law was eventually eroded by judicial decisions, the final liberalization being effected by a court re-interpretation in 1936.

Margaret Sanger's organization was largely supported by women. Marion Bassett, writing in *Women Speaking* (July 1968), states:

I was directly involved in these [Planned Parenthood] activities and attended meetings of the Birth Control Federation of America with several thousand women and only three or four men attending. . . . Margaret Sanger, Dr. Hannah Stone, with many women helping, introduced into Congress year after year for ten years, a proposed change which would allow doctors to give knowledge and materials 'to their patients who needed them for health reasons'. But Congress – 98% of its members being men – never passed this improved legislation. . . . The majority of congressmen went lumbering along in their ignorance or fear of losing the Catholic votes.[7]

Margaret Sanger continued to be active in international birth control circles and became joint president of the International Planned Parenthood Federation in 1952. She died in 1966 and the world press produced a spate of articles acclaiming her work.

There has recently been a resurgence of feminism in America, largely through the influence of Mrs Betty Friedan, President of the National Organization for Women. Mrs Friedan's best-selling book, *The Feminine Mystique* (1963), attacked the belief, based on modern interpretations of Freudian psychology, that women were satisfied with the domestic role allocated to them and content to be educated to adapt themselves to the sphere of wife and mother. As well as demanding implementation of equal pay (the Federal Government has come out in favour of this but State laws vary) and the removal of various restrictions on the part of employers, such as those requiring pregnant employees to resign, the N.O.W. has come out strongly in favour of women having control over family size, which involves the liberalization of the law regarding abortion. At present (August 1969) abortions can be obtained relatively easily in three States only, and here a residential qualification is required.

Mrs Friedan's projected book, *The New Woman*, may well be published before this work and one looks forward to her account of the new-style American feminist.

Notes

1 Shaplen, Robert, *Free Love and Heavenly Sinners*, 1956, 5. See also Johnston, Johanna, *Mrs Satan*, 1967.

2 Sanger, William, *History of Prostitution, its Extent, Causes and Effects throughout the World*, 1919, 584.

3 Russell, Bertrand, *Autobiography*, 1967, i. 124.

4 Blackwell, Emily, *Proceedings of the National Purity Congress,* 14–16.10.1895. Quoted in Sinclair, Andrew, *The Better Half,* 1966, 134.

5 Hay-Cooper, L., *Josephine Butler,* 1922, 270, 401.

6 Goldman, Emma, *Living My Life,* 1932, 553.

7 Bassett, Marion, 'U.S. Women's Struggle for Planned Parenthood' in *Women Speaking,* July 1968, 18–19.

15

The New Woman
and Bachelor Motherhood

If I have freedom in my love
  And in my soul am free,
Angels alone, that soar above,
  Enjoy such liberty.

Richard Lovelace

The 'new woman' emerged in the 1880s, was a feature of the 1890s and endured until the First World War, after which all but the strongest of her representatives were submerged by the roaring 'twenties. She tended to be a radical intellectual, who extended her feminism beyond the claims of the organized women's movement for civil rights to the sphere of sexual ethics. Conventional marriage was found wanting and some of the 'new women' formed unions without benefit of clergy; most were high-minded and believed that men and women, if free of the chains of matrimony, would be likely to form monogamous associations. Many of those who entered into common law marriages suffered considerably, for they were too thin-skinned to undergo conventional disapproval without distress. As well as rejecting the legal bondage of conventional marriage, the new woman viewed with repugnance the possibility of being tied to a man who no longer loved her, or whom she no longer loved. Many were literary figures, such as Olive Schreiner, best known for her *Story of an African Farm* (1883), George Egerton (Mrs Golding Bright), who portrayed the 'woman problem' in fiction and Eleanor Marx (Karl Marx's daughter), who formed an irregular and unsatisfactory union with Edward Aveling. Holding advanced ideas, the new women tended to be freethinkers and neo-Malthusians, but the definition was a loose one and could include Beatrice Webb, in spite of the facts that in her younger days she opposed women's suffrage and that her marriage to Sidney Webb was obviously an example of an ideal partnership. Most women holding advanced ideas or active in public life were apt to be classed as new women, so Annie Besant and Marie Stopes qualified, though the latter's activities came at a time when the idea of the new woman was on the wane, as she could scarcely compete in audacity with the flappers.

Some new women contributed to a rather odd journal, which emerged in 1897, called *The Adult*, described as the 'Journal of the Legitimation League' and, later in 1898, as the 'Journal of Sex'. This journal reported a lecture by Dora F. Kerr to the Legitimation League on March 7th, 1898, entitled 'The Conversion of Mrs Grundy', which roundly condemned contemporary standards. The speaker said:

> We profess ignorance in children, entire sex suppression in girls and youths, full-blossomed knowledge and wisdom at the moment of marriage, unrelieved life-long sex-starvation for half the women of the upper class, and deprivation during the most vigorous years in life of the majority of men. There is (fortunately) *some* difference between what is professed and what is actually done. . . . There is a great deal of Free-Love among married people in England, in the refined classes . . . the one great drawback to it is the amount of deceit which endangers self respect. . . . I contend that enforced celibacy is . . . disastrous to a woman. . . . I believe reform in this connection . . . will largely come from the class which has most suffered from the old system. I mean unmarried women. They have everything to gain and nothing to lose. . . . These women will now claim their freedom to have such men friends as seems good to them, and to be on such terms with their friends as seems right to themselves.[1]

To some extent Dora Kerr, and other contributors to *The Adult*, echoed the thought of Dr George Drysdale, who published anonymously, as 'A Doctor of Medicine', a work entitled *Physical, Sexual and Natural Religion* in 1854. Subsequent expanded editions of this book were called *The Elements of Social Science* and went through several editions in many languages. In his book Dr Drysdale supported Malthusianism, explained methods of family limitation, roundly describing the 'three primary social evils' as 'Poverty,

Prostitution and Celibacy'.[2] He referred to 'the utterly selfish views of love which prevail among us' and added, 'The want of love is indeed fearfully felt in every grade of our society, but by no class so much as by young ladies.'[3]

A later issue of *The Adult* (June 1898) had an advertisement directed to 'The Girls Who Do', inviting applications for a vacancy in a shorthand-writer's office. The editor apparently felt it necessary to comment that he could answer for the *bona fides* of the advertiser. Perhaps, after all, the girls didn't, or at least thought this was not the way to arrange matters, for it was necessary to re-advertise the following month. This time the advertisement was no longer to 'The Girls Who Do' and the editor's reassurance was also omitted. The next month's issue contained no such advertisement, so presumably the place was filled. The expression comes from Grant Allan's book, *The Woman Who Did*, published in 1895, and the March 1898 issue of *The Adult* included 'A Note on the Woman Who Did'. Enquiries concerning free love were received by the editor, who answered a correspondent in August 1898: 'Enquirer – Oh dear no; free love is not illegal, – the illegality consists in discussing its merits, that is all'.[4]

Another example of the new woman was Isadora Duncan (1878–1927), who developed a free form of dancing in flowing robes, rejecting the conventional restrictions of women's clothing, as well as conventional morals. Born an American, her reputation was international.

The species was, of course, to be found in America and included Margaret Sanger. Perhaps the archtype was Emma Goldman, whom we have already met in connection with birth control and who is remembered, amongst other things, for her remark that 'women need not always keep their mouths shut and their wombs open'. The importance to feminism of Emma Goldman lies in her belief that the vote, when obtained, and other conventional feminist objectives regarding civil rights and the right to work, would not be enough to bring emancipation unless women claimed freedom over their own bodies. By this she meant freedom from the legal bondage of marriage, freedom to love where she would, and, in particular, the right to decide whether and when to have children. Emma considered that, through marriage, a woman became a lifelong dependant and this inhibited her personal development. She blamed women as much as men for this state of affairs, feeling they were misguided in centring all their hopes on the vote and that their conventionality and puritanism prevented them from claiming happiness and freedom. She was in advance of her time in her beliefs that the demands of the flesh should be satisfied and that sexual fulfilment should practically be looked upon as a human right. A believer in free love, she acted on her belief but emerges, on the whole, as a motherly figure (though a somewhat formidable one), rather than a *femme fatale*. The driving force of her life was her social conscience, which took the form of the pursuit of freedom through the anarchist movement. Although feminist, her beliefs put her outside the main feminist movement; she was nevertheless eminently a 'new woman'.

In Europe, Rosa Luxemburg (1870–1919) was an outstanding figure. Socialism dominated her life and her marriage to Gustav Lubeck, the son of a friend, was a matter of form, entered into in order to obtain German nationality. (She had been born in Russian Poland, of a Jewish merchant family.) Unlike Emma Goldman, she showed little interest in the position of women, but true to her socialist convictions, looked upon her association with her fellow-socialist, Leo Jogiches, as a private matter. She was largely responsible for drafting the programme of the German Communist party after the First World War and her political importance is such that one hesitates to include her amongst the new women. Few women have been important enough to be murdered for their political convictions, as she was, together with Karl Liebknecht, in 1919.

To revert to England and a much smaller scale of events, the new woman was subjected to attacks from her own sex almost as soon as she emerged, as well as from men. Prominent amongst female antagonists were Mrs Humphrey Ward and Mrs E. Lynn Linton, the latter dubbing the species, 'the Wild Women'. Attack, defence and counter-attack ran through the pages of the Journals, such as the *Nineteenth Century*, in which Mrs Lynn Linton complained (October 1891), 'She (the Wild Woman) smokes after dinner with the men; in railway carriages, in public rooms – when she is allowed,' and (July 1891), 'Marriage, in its old-fashioned aspect as the union of two lives, they repudiate as a one-sided tyranny; and maternity, for which, after all, women primarily exist, they regard as degradation.'

Bachelor motherhood may be looked upon as having developed from the ideology of the new woman. After the First World War, the idea spread amongst certain feminists in Britain, Australia and the U.S.A. that they should claim the right to motherhood without marriage. Several factors contributed to this development. In part it was a gesture of independence and in part a protest against the law relating to the guardianship of infants, which vested control of children mainly in the father. It was argued that the only way for a woman to have control of her own child or children was to be unmarried. The slaughter of men in the war and consequent shortage of potential husbands contributed to the growth of the movement. Eugenic motives were also present; it was felt that an intelligent, professional woman should be able to choose a father for her child with desirable physical and mental characteristics, without having to marry him, and that the child of such a union would be a high type of human being. As we know, 'this ain't necessarily so', for Mendelian theory shows there are other possibilities. At the time, marriage and a career were seen as alternatives and it seemed unfair that the professional woman should be expected to renounce maternity as well as marriage. Obviously, it was believed that adequate domestic help would be readily obtainable and could be afforded by the women concerned.

Australian interest was referred to by Marie Stopes in giving evidence during her libel action. In answer to the Lord Chief Justice she stated:

> The author of the system of what is called scientific motherhood in these passages [in *Married Love*] about which I am now asked, is the wife of the Commissioner of Australia, and she has sent me a large number of reports about the Institute which he desired to found.[5]

The Lord Chief Justice enquired, 'Why you thought it necessary to introduce this matter of insemination of a woman with the seed of other men into a book sold broadcast to old and young?' Dr Stopes replied: 'The reason was that I was importuned to do so by important people, but there were other reasons; one of the

Yours very truly,

M. C. Stopes.

9 Marie Stopes *Photograph by Mr G. A. Coral*

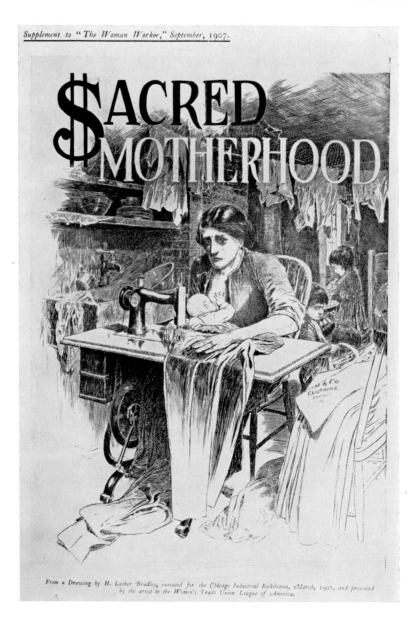

$ACRED MOTHERHOOD

From a Drawing by H. Luther Bradley, executed for the Chicago Industrial Exhibition, March, 1907, and presented by the artist to the Women's Trade Union League of America.

10 'Sacred Motherhood' This drawing of 'sweated labour' illustrates the situation which Margaret Sanger and Marie Stopes sought to alleviate *Bodleian Library, Oxford*

great sources of disappointment and unhappiness in marriage is the failure to have children'.[6]

Here Dr Stopes is obviously referring to artificial insemination in the context of marriage, but there was also interest in this development amongst unmarried women. Dr Stopes's American counterpart, Margaret Sanger, was interested at an early stage in her career and claimed the right of motherhood for unmarried women during the period when she edited the *Woman Rebel*.

Bachelor motherhood was foreshadowed by the works of Ellen Key, whose *Love and Marriage* was published in London in 1911 with an introduction by Havelock Ellis. Ellen Key was a Swedish woman of Scottish ancestry, who was a strong advocate of women's rights and occupied the Chair of History of Civilization at Stockholm University for twenty years. Her reputation was largely based on the popularity of her ideas and work in Germany. It is perhaps no accident that a Swedish woman should have anticipated post-war thought on the issue. One is inclined to feel that the old anti-Corn Law adage that what Manchester thinks today, London thinks tomorrow, could be applied to Sweden and the rest of the Western world in matters of morality, though it cannot be said that Ellen Key's thought was generally acceptable in Sweden in her time. Also, her idea of feminism differed from that current in Anglo-Saxon countries, where the emphasis was on equality with men, for she concentrated on the rights of women as women and their right to be both emancipated and unlike men.

Chapter V of *Love and Marriage* is concerned with 'The Right of Motherhood'. Ellen Key discusses the type of woman to whom motherhood is secondary to the fulfilment of her nature in love and then goes on to refer to 'Those women who are now demanding liberty for motherhood, not only without wedlock but also without love.' She writes:

> The new woman's will to live through herself, with herself, for herself, reaches its limit when she begins to regard men merely as a means to a child. Woman could scarcely take a more complete revenge for having herself been treated for thousands of years as a means.[7]

This attitude is deplored but Ellen Key felt that there should be an opportunity for the single woman, whose life was being blighted through lack of opportunity to express her maternal instinct, to have a child. She wrote:

> Finally, there are exceptional cases, where a superior woman – for it is often the best who are seized by the powerful desire of a child – feels that she cannot combine her motherhood with the claims of love and of intellectual production; that she can suffice for only two duties, and therefore accepts from love the child but renounces marriage.[8]

In the context of the relatively long hours demanded of workers in her day, Ellen Key considered it too difficult to combine work, marriage and motherhood but thought that the woman who must work could combine work and love (i.e. a childless marriage or association) or work and motherhood, though not all these three aspects of life simultaneously.

The post-war claim to bachelor motherhood was to some extent a hangover from the Victorian woman's over-valuation of the emotional satisfaction of motherhood, compared with that of sex. It was not a very practical idea, involving as it did the assumption that cheap, domestic labour would always be available and also exposing the child of the 'bachelor mother' to the scorn of the conventional. The idea soon died a natural death, not only because of the difficulties mentioned but because, to the modern mind, it involved all the pains and troubles of the female state without any of the fun.

Isadora Duncan was what one might term a deliberately unmarried mother but after her first experience of childbirth under somewhat primitive conditions, she concluded that painless childbirth for all women was much more important than the suffrage.

Perhaps the most notable feminist who chose motherhood without marriage was Sylvia Pankhurst. It seems probable that this was an expression of her socialism as well as her feminism and it scarcely comes under the description of bachelor motherhood as her association with the exiled Italian socialist, Silvio Corio, was an enduring one.

Notes

1 Kerr, Dora F., 'The Conversion of Mrs Grundy', in *The Adult*, May 1898, ii. no. 4, 98–101.

2 Drysdale, George, *Physical, Sexual and Natural Religion*, 1872.

3 *Ibid.*, 335.

4 *The Adult*, August 1898, ii. no. 7, 220.

5 Box, Muriel, *The Trial of Marie Stopes*, 1967, 105.

6 *Ibid.*, 106.

7 Key, Ellen, *Love and Marriage*, 1911, 175.

8 *Ibid.*, 192.

16

The Pankhursts, Purity and the Sex War

Celibacy, which tens of thousands of
Englishwomen endure cheerfully, ought
not to be thought miserable by Englishmen.

Professor Francis William Newman

The name of Pankhurst is so closely associated in the public mind with votes for women that the attacks on contemporary morals and the purity crusade by Mrs Pankhurst and Christabel are apt to be overlooked. Mrs Pankhurst's motivation is clear enough but that of Christabel somewhat less so. Like most feminists, they accepted conventional moral standards and deplored the gap between theory and practice. Male supporters of the double standard of morality tended to be anti-suffragist, fearing that women, on gaining political power would insist on a 'clean-up' of the cities; suffragette hostility was, therefore, aroused on double grounds.

In Mrs Pankhurst's case, her attitude was influenced by her experiences as a member of the Chorlton Board of Guardians and her subsequent work, on becoming widowed, as Registrar of Births and Deaths in the Rusholme District of Manchester. Always a compassionate woman, quick to resent injustice, she grieved for the pitiable plight of many of the girls who came to register the births of illegitimate children and felt keenly the difference between their position and that of the fathers of the newborn infants.

In her phase of patriotism following the First World War, Mrs Pankhurst was anxious to support all that was best in the national life, which included, of course, 'high moral standards'. While lecturing in Canada, mainly on an anti-Bolshevist theme, she was recruited as a speaker for the National Council for Combating

Venereal Diseases which had been formed by Dr Gordon Bates, formerly of the Canadian Army Medical Corps. Perhaps it would be more accurate to say that she persuaded Dr Bates to enlist her, as he seems to have been rather nervous about it, but he need not have worried, for this was a theme on which Mrs Pankhurst could speak with a high-minded delicacy and hold an audience. She was so successful that she was able to carve out a new career for herself in Canada and the U.S.A. as the leading lecturer on 'the social disease'.[1] In spite of taking out Canadian citizenship, she found the Canadian winters too grim and, after convalescing in Bermuda, returned to Europe in 1925. Her attitude cannot be taken as typical of all her former colleagues, many of whom were relatively uninterested in personal morals, feeling that private lives should be private. This attitude also partially explains the continuing lack of unanimous feminist support for Josephine Butler's movement. As has been indicated, in the nineteenth century it split the feminists, as one group felt that the odium it attracted was a danger to other feminist causes; in the twentieth century, the attainment of the parliamentary vote became an obsession and many of the campaigners were simply not interested in the moral welfare movement, although practically all believed that the women's vote would lead to a more moral society.

Although supporting high moral standards, Emmeline Pankhurst cannot be looked upon as a man-hater. During the period of her marriage, she had adored her husband. Rebecca West's analysis of her attitude, included in *The Post Victorians* (1933), is interesting:

> Mrs. Pankhurst had sublimated her sex antagonism. She was in no way a man-hater, loving her sons as deeply as her daughters, and she completely converted her desire to offend the other sex into a desire to defend her own.[2]

Even more interesting is Miss West's interpretation of the means whereby Mrs Pankhurst obtained such tremendous influence over so many women. She (Rebecca West) considered this was through provoking male sex-antagonism to open and candid expression and thus making all self-respecting women feel it was something they must fight. Indeed, the claim for women's rights had continuously produced much ribaldry inside and outside Parliament; the

suggestion that a future woman Lord Chancellor might be seized
with labour pains on the Woolsack was thought so amazingly funny,
as was anything connected with childbirth. Women around the
age of forty-five were, of course, considered out of their minds –
a myth not yet killed stone dead. Rebecca West's thesis deserves
attention not only as an explanation of the Pankhurst magic, which
is usually attributed to Mrs Pankhurst's powers as a public speaker,
but also for the implication that sex hostility amongst women was
largely absent or latent until provoked by male insults. According
to Miss West, Emmeline Pankhurst realized many women would
come out in support of women's rights if they knew what men really
thought of them.

The case of Christabel Pankhurst is less easy to understand.
Though subject to insult, as were all the suffragettes, there would
seem to be no basic reason why she should take up the question of
masculine morals and venereal disease. She was a good-looking
and successful woman, admired by Frederick Pethick Lawrence and
other male supporters of the movement, as well as by her fellow
suffragettes. The immediately predisposing cause of Christabel's
'anti-men' outburst in 1913 was the Piccadilly Flat Case and the
contrast between the sentence of three months' imprisonment im-
posed on the procuress Queenie Gerald, and the three years' imprisonment to which her mother had been sentenced. Also, Queenie
had been put in the second division, while Annie Kenney, her
(Christabel's) lieutenant, was in the third division with other
suffragettes.

The Piccadilly Flat Case was revealed at the Marlborough Street
Police Court and London Sessions in June and July 1913, and extensively publicized by the *Globe* newspaper. Though unpleasant,
involving the prostitution of girls not much over the age of consent
and the discovery of birches and other instruments of flagellation
in the flat in question, it was nothing out of the ordinary in the
history of prostitution but was one of those cases which was
seized upon by the public with avidity, one imagines in much
the same way as the trial of Stephen Ward at the time of the
Profumo affair. Also, the case aroused disquiet through the very
general feeling on the part of the public that a 'whitewashing'
operation had been undertaken to protect men in high places.

Queenie Gerald's real name was not published, nor the names of her customers. At the London Sessions on July 10th, the Chairman (Mr A. J. Lawrie) ordered the court to be cleared, with the exception of a few privileged persons and some of the press, and asked the press not to publish names. Although the court had been cleared on account of the alleged indecency of the case, he did not ask for details to be withheld, only names. Keir Hardie attacked the Government in the House of Commons on the conduct of the case and also for not prosecuting Queenie Gerald as a procuress; he maintained that she had not been charged with procuring, as her defence would have been that she had acted as an agent and the names now being concealed would necessarily have been revealed. 'Therefore, the whole plot to conceal and shield the men who were the principal guilty parties in this affair made it impossible to proceed with the charge of the woman being a procuress.'[3]

Christabel Pankhurst wrote a series of articles in *The Suffragette* (the W.S.P.U. newspaper which had succeeded *Votes for Women* after the break with the Pethick Lawrences), subsequently published in book form as *The Great Scourge and How to End It*.[4] The scourge was venereal disease, the incidence amongst men being supported with exaggerated statistics obtained from medical men who, presumably, were either scaremongering or not very good at statistics. The titles of the articles, or chapters as they appear in the book, speak for themselves and include one entitled 'The End of a Great Conspiracy' and two on 'The Dangers of Marriage'. The theme was that the 'scourge' could be ended by 'chastity for men', which, in any event, was good for them, and 'votes for women', because women, when enfranchised, would no longer endure a situation where prostitution was rampant and cases like the Piccadilly Flat Case could arise. Subsequent and, indeed, some contemporary feminists felt Christabel's outburst, implying that men were monsters, was unfortunate when the drive for equality should be leading to more comradely relations between men and women. The constitutional leader, Mrs Fawcett, always endeavoured to check 'anti-man' sentiment amongst her followers, but there was a fundamental difference in policy between the constitutionalists and the militants. As the co-operation of a male parliament was necessary to obtain the vote, Mrs Fawcett was always anxious to provide face-saving opportunities for her antagonists to change their minds, as well as genuinely disbelieving in a 'sex war', while the militants proceeded by applying pressure on the Government and making the lives of cabinet ministers thoroughly uncomfortable so long as they opposed women's suffrage. Both movements played their part in the eventual attainment of the vote.

Whatever view one takes of Christabel's crusade for purity, the historian of the women's movement must be grateful to find in her outburst a plain summary of a largely concealed source of bitterness in the background of feminism. The protest against the double standard of morality was not just an abstract protest against injustice nor was it motivated by jealousy of the greater freedom of men; it derived its force through many individual married women making the discovery that there were diseases of which their upbringing had left them in ignorance and of which they were in personal risk of infection through male recourse to prostitutes. Though the social causes of the situation were much more complex than many of the purity campaigners realized, the reaction of resentment against the situation was a reasonable and logical reaction, not a neurotic or pathological one. For a spouse of either sex to feel resentment at being exposed to infection through the activity of his or her marriage partner is, surely, entirely comprehensible.

Christabel, in her somewhat unfortunate tirade, the tenor of which was already outdated, was not voicing sentiments approved by women only; she received considerable support from the clergy and, indeed, had been anticipated in 1907 by the Rev R. J. Campbell, who spoke on 'Women's Suffrage and The Social Evil'[5] on December 17th of that year, under the auspices of the Men's League for Women's Suffrage.

The present would seem to be as good a place as any to examine the charge that the feminists were man-haters, for this is largely based on Josephine Butler's attitude, Christabel's stepping-up of the sex war, and the reference made by George Dangerfield in *The Strange Death of Liberal England* (1936) to an outbreak of lesbianism amongst the suffragettes in 1912.[6] To take the last reference first, the accusation is not supported with any evidence, though it obviously might have been embarrassing, with so many of the suffragettes alive, to have produced any evidence available. I can only say that in seven years of studying the feminist movement, at one period, with particular reference to the suffragettes, I have never come across such evidence either in writing or through private enquiry. Before commencing this book, I approached certain leading suffragettes on the subject, one of whom (who was closely associated with Christabel Pankhurst and at the heart of affairs) made the sensible comment that although, amongst the thousands of women attached to the movement, there may well have been some lesbians, she had seen nothing to indicate this. George Dangerfield's book is so greatly valued by sociologists as showing insight concerning the pressures leading to the outbreak of lawlessness in the years before the First World War (though historians are not quite so unanimous in their verdict) that it seems a pity the suggestion of lesbianism amongst the suffragettes should be perpetuated in successive editions of this well-known book and quoted in at least one other standard work, namely, *Feminism and Family Planning in Victorian England*, by J. A. and Olive Banks (p. 113), unless it can be substantiated as anything in excess of what would be normal in the population as a whole. On the one hand, a women's organization would obviously provide the opportunity for forming attachments between women and might attract those predisposed in this direction, but, on the other hand, adherents of the movement were almost excessively high-minded and looked upon their cause as one directed towards a better society with a high moral tone. The charge against the main groups of feminists, at least until the First World War, is that they supported the rigid code of Victorian morality rather than claiming for women emotional and sexual freedom as well as civil rights. In demanding as Christabel did, 'Votes for women and chastity for men', women's chastity was taken for granted. Perhaps, however, George Dangerfield did not mean the term 'lesbianism' to be taken literally. He states:

And it was from some secret yearning to recover the wisdom of women that the homosexual movement first manifested itself, in 1912, among the suffragettes. . . . It possibly deserves every bad epithet but one – it was not perverse. People very frequently damn the sins they have no mind to, whether in sex or literature or politics, by calling them perverse; but perversity, if it means anything at all, means the conscious and deliberate preference of something low before something high, of death before life. And this pre-war lesbianism – which, in any case, was more sensitive than sensual – was without any question a striving towards life.[7]

If, in fact, the strong *esprit de corps* which had developed amongst the suffragettes is all that is meant, why call it lesbianism or homosexuality? Surely group solidarity, though commoner amongst men than with women, is not a male prerogative?

The 'anti-man' charge is not easy to analyse. While support for it can be found, the difficulty arises that the feminists could hardly challenge male supremacy without attacking men. The question arises, also, whether anti-male sentiments were in any way comparable in volume to the mass of derogatory statements by men concerning women. This raises the interesting question of why it is considered a heinous offence for a woman to dislike men but (at least, until recently) has been quite acceptable, even creditable, for a man to say he 'has no time for women'.

The 'anti-man' charge is largely based on some statements of Josephine Butler, quoted below, and on Christabel Pankhurst's attitude in 1913, already discussed. In the endeavour to find additional material, other than the usual attacks on the injustice of male privilege made in feminist literature, I consulted the Fawcett Librarian, enquiring if there was anything under a library classification of 'man-haters', 'anti-man', or anything similar; I was told (after a search) that there was not, with the unsolicited comment, 'Of course, there is plenty of the opposite.'

As has been mentioned earlier, Mrs Butler was strongly opposed to vice and would express her outrage at cases she came across of girls who had been seduced and abandoned or tricked into resorting to a house of ill-fame, tending to see women as victims most of the time. It is, however, her statement in a letter to a friend about to be confined, in 1893, which seems to be taken as particularly indicative of her attitude to men.

> I know it must be very horrid to go, as it were, a beast to the shambles; and I wish you had a motherly friend near you. But your ever faithful God is near you, dear. You remember how sweet and lovely Jesus always was to *women*, and how he helped their *woman* diseases, and how respectful he was to them and loved them and

forgave the sins of the most sinful. And he was born of a woman –
a woman only. No man had any hand in *that*. It was such a favour
to women.[8]

It is presumably the reference to Christ being born of woman only,
without any man having a hand in it, that gives rise to the suggestion
that Mrs Butler was antagonistic to men, but surely the passage
quoted is capable of an alternative interpretation. Here is a very
religious woman, believing literally in the virgin birth, trying to
find consolation for a friend about to undergo a confinement under
the medical conditions of Victorian times, possibly without an
anaesthetic. The word 'shambles' is not entirely inappropriate. One
counts one's blessings when things are in a bad state and the woman
in question was about to suffer some of the pains of the female condition. Mrs Butler sought to provide her friend with some compen-
sations for being a woman and naturally turned to her religion.

There are revealing passages in L. Hay-Cooper's biography of
Josephine Butler (1922). He quotes her as follows:

> As I grew up, I became quite melancholy at what seemed to me a
> perpetual injustice crushing woman. You have no idea how bitter
> this made me as a girl. Then came my marriage . . . and softened my
> bitterness. . . . Do not . . . for a moment suppose I am attributing to
> men any *intentional* injustice.[9]

Mrs Butler believed in the co-education of girls and boys and that
the two sexes would rise or fall together. Her attitude, as expressed
in answers to the Royal Commission on the Contagious Diseases
Acts, has already been discussed in an earlier chapter, but it is perhaps worth quoting the following additional evidence, given on
March 17th, 1871: 'As mothers of sons we [women] demand to
know what the influence of these [C.D.] Acts is on young men'
(Qn. 12,869).

To the question of whether she thought prostitutes were always
tempted into a career of vice by seduction she replied: 'Decidedly
not. . . . In Liverpool . . . there is a mass of people, boys and girls,
who begin to be unchaste and vicious from their earliest years'
(Qn. 12,879). On the subject of why girls went 'on the town', she
was asked: 'Some from wantonness?' and answered, 'No doubt.'
(Qn. 12,884).

A decade later she was still referring to herself as a mother of sons when giving evidence to the House of Commons Select Committee. On May 5th, 1882, she was asked: 'You have made it your business to study this matter with a view to reclaiming the women?' she replied: 'And with a view to reclaiming men quite as much' (Qn. 5,375). In spite of her tendency to see women as victims, Josephine Butler's attitude was not entirely unrelated to that of Millicent Fawcett, who considered that so long as men had daughters and women had sons, a sex war was impossible.

One would not dispute that an element of hostility against men showed itself from time to time in the feminist movement; the question is, rather, whether this was the natural and reasonable reaction of an underprivileged group or whether, as the anti-feminists contended, it was neurotic and pathological in its nature. Here some comparative material would be helpful, such as an analysis of class warfare and racial hatred. Without having undertaken such an analysis, I venture to suggest that the expression of sex antagonism has been considerably less extreme than that of class or racial hatred, being offset by sex attraction and by the reluctance of most married women to push their claims to the extent of endangering domestic harmony. Feminists pushed their claims and men opposed them, but the former always had male champions and female opponents. The sex war was a phoney war. Nevertheless, the feminists tended to assert that women were morally superior to men, a claim that American males were prepared to grant.

There is a vast amount of disparaging literature on women, produced both before and after the feminist movement, but this does not prove anything very much regarding sex antipathy. What it mainly does is to illustrate that men were the dominant sex, were more literate than women and could afford to be offensive if they felt like it. The wickedness of women, their very existence being a temptation of the flesh, is a familiar theme, with roots in Judaism and early Christianity, and persisted until the idea of feminine purity took hold in the nineteenth century. There is little profit in going back to ancient arguments as to whether women have souls or not. The misogynist is a familiar character and many derogatory comments are well known, such as that of Dr Johnson that 'A woman's preaching is like a dog's walking on his hinder legs. It is not done well; but you are surprised to find it done at all.' Misogyny is a well-established English word. What is its converse? Misoandry? One cannot find this, or anything similar, in English dictionaries. English literature is not exceptional; as Simone de Beauvoir has stated, 'We are familiar with the savage indictments hurled against women throughout French literature.'[10] With so much disparagement a commonplace before the development of the women's movement provoked additional hostility, it is not surprising to find that a flood of abuse descended on the feminists, once they staked their claim.

I have discussed anti-feminist attitudes in an earlier work on the women's suffrage campaign,[11] under the headings of 'The Arguments Used' and 'The Anti-Suffragists'; perhaps the clearest expression of such attitudes is to be found in Sir Almroth E. Wright's letter to *The Times* of March 28th, 1912, and subsequent book (in which this letter is incorporated as an Appendix) entitled *The Unexpurgated Case against Woman Suffrage*.[12] As a physician and surgeon, Sir Almroth assumed an expert knowledge of woman's physiological and psychological make-up, apparently, extended to her moral nature. He wrote, *inter alia*, of 'Women's disability in the matter of intellect', 'Distortions in woman's mental picture of life, and lacunae in that of "spinsters of retarded development"', 'Difference between man and woman in matters of public morality' and 'Problem presented by the physiological psychology of woman'. One is relieved to find that the final section has been summarized as 'Peace will come when surplus women shall have been removed by emigration'. We are indebted to Sir Almroth (in the same way as to Christabel Pankhurst) for setting out clearly a theme underlying the school of thought he represented and which is expressed in different ways in various speeches and writings. In addition to the implication that women were neither physically nor mentally capable of becoming full human beings is the idea of an implicit contract between men and women, to the effect that men, who had the power, would afford courtesy and protection to women so long as (and only so long as) women kept their share of the bargain, which was to acknowledge male superiority and, above all, not to resort to physical force. The whole suffrage campaign, particularly suffragettes' scuffles with the police, was a breach of this contract between the sexes. As we have already seen, the contract was some-what limited in application, having little relevance to the poorer section of the community. According to Sir Almroth:

> When a man makes this compact with a woman, 'I will do you reverence, and protect you, and yield you service' . . . it is not a question of a purely one-sided bargain. . . . the contract is in-fringed when woman breaks out in violence; when she jettisons her personal refinement; when she is ungrateful; and, possibly, when she places a quite extravagantly high estimate upon her intellectual powers.[13]

To the charge that some feminists were man-haters, one can make the counter-charge that there is ample evidence of woman-hatred; while both attitudes are to be deplored, it does not seem reasonable to assert that the former was in excess of the latter.

Perhaps the answer to the question of why it has been looked upon as so much worse for women to dislike men than the converse is the belief that the sole justification for the existence of women is that they should be wives (or at least sexual partners) and mothers. If this is so, it would provide a partial explanation of the dislike of spinsters which seems to emerge at times. In the nineteenth and part of the current century the 'female supernumeraries' or 'surplus women' – derogatory terms in themselves – have at times been treated not only as an economic burden but as if they had no right to exist. As Byron put it:

> Man's love is of man's life a thing apart,
> 'Tis woman's whole existence.

The idea persists that a man's life is justified by his contribution to the work of the world and if he chooses to remain unmarried (as, for instance, has the current leader of the Conservative Party, Mr Edward Heath), it is his own affair. In the case of an unmarried woman her social contribution has to be of marked and obvious usefulness, such as that of a nurse, for her unmarried state to receive social approval. This attitude was particularly unfair during the period when there was an excess of women over men in the marriage-able age groups (no longer the case in modern Britain) and it was statistically impossible for all women to marry.

It has been claimed above that the sex war was a phoney war but perhaps this should be modified by saying, as the late Professor Joad might have put it, that it all depends on what one means by 'the sex war'. There was certainly no sex war in the sense of widespread hatred of men by women, but if by 'war' one means a somewhat diffused campaign or movement by women to escape from conventional limitations and attain the position of full human beings, this is something which has many aspects and is still going on. In addition to the organized campaigns for civil rights which reached their apex in the years before the First World War and the current campaign for equal pay, there is a largely submerged protest movement, given expression to, when it surfaces, mainly by literary figures. This movement, if anything with such vaguely formulated objectives can be dignified by the term, is a protest against being looked upon as 'the incidental, the inessential as opposed to the essential', as Simone de Beauvoir puts it in her introduction to *The Second Sex*. While denying the possibility of any cleavage along the lines of sex, in other words, of a sex war, Mme de Beauvoir highlights the general assumption that, 'A man is in the right in being a man; it is the woman who is in the wrong.'[14] Somewhat similar protests have been made in most Western countries; the title of Marya Mannes's article in the *New York Times Magazine*, 'Female Intelligence, Who Wants it?'[15] speaks for itself. Margaret Mead's comment on the 1968 situation in America is that, 'The only way a woman can marry now is to agree to become a charwoman, regardless of her education and skills.' In an interesting broadcast (reproduced in *The Listener* of October 10th, 1968) Angus Wilson traces the sex war through the English novel, from the eighteenth century to the present day, noting the recession of the Victorian idea of the woman as a victim and hoping that the sexual revolution, introduced by the younger generation, will be successful enough to prevent intelligent women from adopting an attitude similar to that of the Black Power group. The emergence of a female equivalent of Black Power would seem unlikely for several reasons. There has been a reaction against the Pankhurst type of feminism or, at least, the popular image of it, and most women value the greater comradeship currently existing between men and women. Also, the criticisms levied by women are directed against their own sex as much as against the opposite sex; women should make greater efforts, it is contended, to realize their full potentialities and are as much at fault in accepting an inferior role as men are in allocating it to them. Apart from equal pay, which needs adopting in some countries including Britain and implementing effectively in countries where it has been formally adopted, the lack of definite objectives in countries where legal equality has largely been obtained militates against organized feminist campaigns. While women's organizations are far from being inactive, much of the work remaining to be done may well have to be effected by the individual efforts of both men and women to bring the problems into the open and through the determination of individual women to take for granted a higher status than has customarily been accorded to them.

Notes

1 Cf. Mitchell, David, *The Fighting Pankhursts*, 1967.

2 West, Rebecca, *The Post Victorians*, 1933, 485.

3 H.C. Deb., 5S, Vol. LVI, c. 2341. See also cc. 2338–40, 2389–90, 2395–6.

4 Pankhurst, Christabel, *The Great Scourge and How to End It*, 1913.

5 Campbell, R. J., *Women's Suffrage and the Social Evil*, 1907.

6 Dangerfield, George, *The Strange Death of Liberal England*, 1966, 128.

7 *Ibid.*

8 Butler, A. S. G., *Portrait of Josephine Butler*, 1954, 58–9. Cf. also McGregor, O. R., *Divorce in England*, 1957, 91.

9 Hay-Cooper, L., *Josephine Butler*, 1922, 31.

10 De Beauvoir, Simone (trans. H. M. Parshley), *The Second Sex*, 1953, 21.

11 Rover, Constance, *Women's Suffrage and Party Politics in Britain 1866–1914*, 1967, Chapters V and IX.

12 Wright, Almroth E., *The Unexpurgated Case against Woman Suffrage*, 1913.

13 *Ibid.*, 19–20.

14 De Beauvoir, *op. cit.*, 15–16.

15 Mannes, Marya, 'Female Intelligence: Who Wants It?' in *New York Times Magazine*, 8.1.1960. Reprinted in Schnur, E. M. (ed.), *The Family and the Sexual Revolution*, 1966.

11 Mrs Emmeline Pankhurst, Founder of the W.S.P.U.
Fawcett Library, London

12 Christabel Pankhurst, Leader of the W.S.P.U.
Fawcett Library, London

17

Feminism and Modern Morality

*So here we are, with our equal moral
standard stabilized at the lower level,
and a newly established claim of the
female partner to sex satisfaction.*

Mary Stocks

The great moral problems of Victorian times are with us today in a modified form and on the assumption that modern, liberal standards are an advance on the Victorian code, one must try, in this final section, to make some assessment of the contribution of feminism, directly or indirectly, to this improvement. The feminists have been taken to mean those persons, both men and women, who put forward or supported the demand for women's rights and it will have been seen that two main types have emerged. On the one hand there are those, such as Richard Carlile and Emma Goldman, who included feminism in a complex of advanced ideas, usually of a markedly left-wing stamp, directed towards social reform; this group included socialists who looked upon the wedding ring as woman's badge of servitude and who felt, as Lenin was eventually to phrase it, that women must be delivered from the necessity of spending three-quarters of their lives 'in the stinking kitchen'. Members of this group might well have other objectives, such as freedom of speech, socialism or anarchism, which took precedence over feminism in their scale of values. On the other hand there were those, particularly women but not excluding men such as Lord Pethick Lawrence, who formed and supported the organizations which campaigned for civil rights and associated feminist objectives. Amongst the women involved, relatively few belonged to the first group, which included the more extreme of the new women and several 'loners'. There was a certain tendency for the women who were prepared personally to defy the moral code, such as Georges Sand, to be what is usually termed 'men's women'. The bulk of the women who supported the constitutional movement for women's suffrage and other aspects of the women's rights movement in the nineteenth century, and who joined the militant movement in the twentieth century, accepted conventional morality; they also had that sense of sex solidarity which enabled them to form effective pressure groups. It has been noted that the women's organizations in Britain gave somewhat belated recognition to family planning as an integral part of women's freedom.

Since Victorian days middle-class morality, as it affects women, has suffered a major defeat in one direction; it is no longer possible to 'lock up your daughters'. The internal combustion engine has completed the process started by the humble bicycle and made chaperonage impossible; the growth of contraceptive and medical knowledge has made it possible to have sexual experience without the penalties of illegitimate children and disease; in addition, the affluent society has largely removed young people from the parental home. The change has given young women greater freedom, accompanied, of course, by certain risks but the lowering of the age of marriage, due to greater affluence and the likelihood of both partners working until they feel the time is ripe to start a family, has had a limiting effect on girls' education and training. While, in absolute terms, women are better educated than they used to be, a comparison between the training and education of young men and young women today shows the extent to which the expectation of early marriage limits the willingness of the girls themselves, their parents and their employers, to undertake or provide higher education and training, or even sixth-form schooling. The enemy now is not so much the dictates of conventional morality keeping middle-class girls at home and the denial of any but menial positions to working-class women, so much as the disincentive to an effort which may well seem unproductive in view of the short period of work-anticipation before marriage. A university degree still has its attractions as a general education and status symbol, also as a 'launching base' for possible later endeavours, but a minority only of the population is graduate material and prolonged vocational training may well seem pointless in a world where techniques become out-of-date within a five-year period. This is not, of course, to dispute that more provision should be made for the education of girls and women and feminist influence is, rightly, behind efforts in this direction, particularly the endeavours to provide training for older women wishing to re-enter the labour market when children no longer require the full-time presence of their mother in the home.

Another marked change since Victorian times is the growth of the belief that a woman has the right to a satisfactory sex-life. On the face of it, this does not necessarily lead to a change in morality but simply to marital adjustment, but this is to over-simplify the issue. If the belief that it is natural and desirable to have satisfactory sexual experience is stronger than the belief that conventional moral standards should be observed, the likelihood of women (other than prostitutes) indulging in pre-marital or extra-marital *affaires* is increased.

Middle-class morality, however, may be said to have survived for, as Professor O. R. McGregor has pointed out, the rule is still the same as a hundred years ago, namely, no sex outside marriage.[1] Departure from the rule by women, particularly before marriage, is not taken as seriously as used to be the case and there are obviously certain sub-cultures where it does not apply at all. Also, the rule is being increasingly questioned and magazines and Sunday papers tend to run articles enquiring whether marriage as an institution is on the way out, usually including interviews with fairly well-known people who have opted for an unofficial union. For instance, the March 1967 number of *Nova* was advertised in *Sunday Times* (12.3.67) and elsewhere with captions reading, 'Yes, we're living in sin. No, we're not getting married. Why? It's out of date.' *The Observer* colour supplement of September 17th, 1967, featured 'Are we the last married generation?' and the September 1968 issue of *The Plain Truth* was advertised in the *Sunday Times* colour supplement under the heading of 'Marriage soon obsolete?' In spite of this, marriage is more popular than ever, increasing affluence combining with other factors, such as earlier maturity and the disappearance of surplus women in the marriageable age groups, to bring down the age of marriage and encourage a greater proportion of the population than ever before to enter into the state of matrimony. Within marriage, much of the double standard of morality has disappeared and wives are no longer expected to put up with conduct on the part of their husbands which could never for a moment be condoned in themselves.

Society seems to be feeling its way towards a moral code based on social need, as a morality based on religion, convention and the fear of unwanted pregnancy is becoming increasingly unacceptable. Dr Alex Comfort has described changing attitudes towards sexual morality as follows:

> With the growth of knowledge and of rationalism the ground
> shifted, no less in medical than in religious and moralistic writings.
> What was sinful and leading to damnation became deadly and pro-
> ductive of cancer and insanity; then unhealthy, and a cause of muddy
> complexion, poor wind and bags under the eyes – and finally 'im-
> mature' and a sign of low moral fibre, if not of neurosis.[2]

There is a desire to discard such irrational and negative justifications of the moral code and to seek something more positive. This positive justification is found in the need for a stable environment for the rearing of children which, in our culture, can only be found in the family: we are unlikely, in the foreseeable future, to introduce the commune or the kibbutz. The continuing and increasing popularity of marriage is evidence that it satisfies a variety of human needs and aspirations, such as one may find outlined in any reasonable study on the subject,[3] but the need to adhere to unsatisfactory unions which are childless or where the children of the marriage have left the matrimonial home is increasingly questioned, as is the value of a totally unsatisfactory marriage even if there are children. More knowledge is needed and at last we have social scientists, such as sociologists, sexologists and psychologists, who, through the use of modern survey and statistical techniques, are endeavouring to obtain the necessary basis of information on which a rational moral and social code could be grounded.

The contribution of the feminists to the present more liberal situation is largely indirect. Their successful efforts to obtain legal equality and civil rights for women must have had an effect on the position of the married woman, even if still financially dependent upon her husband, and have contributed to the increasingly egalitarian climate of modern thought. Their attacks on the double standard of morality showed up the hypocrisy of the social code and contributed to the elimination of double standards from our divorce laws.

Perhaps the greatest contribution to the personal freedom of married women came more or less 'out of the blue' through a judicial decision. The case of Regina *v* Jackson in 1891 (see Chapter 4) established that a wife was no longer the property of her husband and the latter could not use physical force to keep her in his house. At the time, few unhappy wives were in a position to take advantage of this new personal freedom (unless their husbands wanted to get rid of them), for they were tied through financial dependence and, often, the needs of young children. However, the legal foundation was laid; the increasing actual or potential economic independence of women, to which the feminists contributed through their pressure for the education of girls and the expansion of work opportunities, combined with the smaller family, made it no longer necessary to tolerate the intolerable.

Feminist efforts relating to marriage and divorce have been directed towards financial rather than moral matters (if, for the moment, one ignores double moral standards). The campaign for married women's separate property, established piecemeal in the 1870s and consolidated in 1882, did much to give women financial independence, if they had money through inheritance or earnings, and it has already been contended that personal freedom is related to economic independence. The ability of a wife, if the worst comes to the worst, simply to 'walk out', is basic to freedom of person and as the twentieth century has progressed, this has been made more possible by increased opportunities for employment and the cushion of the welfare state.

Regarding divorce, feminists today find themselves in a difficult position, liberal principles pulling in a different direction from presumed economic interest. With some exceptions, there is support for the proposal, embodied in the Divorce Reform Bills of 1967 and 1968 and subsequently enacted in the Divorce Reform Act, 1969, that the breakdown of marriage should be grounds for the dissolution of the union, even against the wishes of the innocent party, provided something is done to safeguard a divorced woman's financial position, particularly with regard to pension rights. This attitude is based both on the merits of the case and the indignity of a woman holding on to a husband who does not want her. There was some feminist support, but quite a lot of opposition, to Baroness Summerskill's description of the (1967) Bill as a 'Casanova's Charter'. Lady Summerskill objected to the provision whereby breakdown of marriage could be established by, *inter alia*, five years' separation, on the application of one party without the consent of the other, contending that this would enable a married man to make a proposal to a second woman with a definite date for marriage and for the legitimation of any children.[4] On the other hand, Dame Joan Vickers, Chairman of the Status of Women Committee and M.P. for Plymouth, Devonport, is reported as stating that she represented twenty-three women's organizations and disputed the claim that women were against the (1968) Divorce Reform Bill.[5] In the House of Commons on December 17th, 1968, she said that 'The Bill would create more happiness for most people than the present conditions and would enable them to lead more honest lives if they wished to separate.'[6] The root of the difficulty, of course (apart from religious opposition), is that women are the economically weaker sex and there is no immediate prospect of this being changed. This might not matter so much if a reasonable minimum income could be obtained relatively easily, but to the difficulties of the interrupted career and domestic obligations are added the handicaps of unequal pay and promotion prospects (in part related to the interrupted career and the tendency amongst women to give priority to family obligation) and the lack of training facilities for middle-aged women who wish to re-enter the labour market. In addition, there are less tangible factors contributing to the economic disadvantage of women, such as the lack of confidence felt by so many of them as the result of their social conditioning. Mrs Lena Jeger emphasized this point in the House of Commons on December 6th, 1968, when Mr Alec Jones moved the Second Reading of the Divorce Reform Bill which, he said, 'was substantially the same as the Bill which emerged from standing committee last session'.[7] In the debate, Mrs Jeger said:

> Most of the difficulties arose from matters which were not part of divorce law. There were no sensible arrangements for married

women in the country's national insurance machinery. Such a woman should have an economic status of her own. She hoped women's organizations would not persist in saying there could not be divorce reform because of the economic dependence of women. There should be a campaign for better economic status for the married woman.[8]

Clause 5 of the Bill places the burden of proof of grave financial or other hardship on the spouse opposing the application for divorce, an undertaking which could well prove difficult and expensive.

Legislation was subsequently proposed to meet the financial objections raised against the 1968 Bill. The Government indicated that divorced women's needs would be taken into account in its new social security plan and a Matrimonial Property Bill, with all-party backing, was introduced, providing for the equal division of matrimonial property between husband and wife in the event of divorce or death. The sponsor of the Bill, Mr Edward Bishop, said that the measure was meant to complement the Divorce Reform Bill and Lady Summerskill indicated that she would drop her opposition to the Divorce Bill, should the Matrimonial Property Bill be passed. The Married Women's Association and the National Council of Women supported the Matrimonial Property Bill, thus underlining the fact that feminist opposition to the divorce measure was on economic rather than moral grounds. The Matrimonial Property Bill, having passed its Second Reading on January 24th, 1969, was withdrawn on the Lord Chancellor's assurance that the Government would introduce legislation on matrimonial financial relief early in the following session. This promise has been kept.

Reverting to the Divorce Reform Act, 1969, it seems to be taken for granted that it will always be the woman who will oppose divorce under the five years' separation provision; perhaps this may not be the case, as married women now comprise over one-sixth of our total labour force. Unless there is a substantial revision of the law regarding matrimonial property, no doubt this will usually be so, for as Sir Jocelyn Simon (President of the Divorce Court) had occasion to state when addressing the Holdsworth Club, 'The cock bird can feather his nest precisely because he is not required to spend most of his time sitting on it.'[9]

The Josephine Butler Society and the International Abolitionist

Federation (the former being an affiliate of the latter) are still an integral part of feminism, with relatively unchanged objectives. At the twenty-first triennial congress of the International Alliance of Women held in London in 1967, five days were devoted to the reports of the Alliance's five standing commissions, one of which was on Equal Moral Standards. An accession of strength was received from the Status of Women Committee, which had previously banned the discussion of prostitution but had lifted the ban at their twentieth session in the spring of 1967 and had included in a draft *Declaration on Discrimination against Women:* Article 8: 'All appropriate measures including legislation shall be taken to combat all forms of traffic in women and exploitation of women.'[10]

The idea of woman as a victim dies hard, perhaps because women may still be victims, particularly in underdeveloped countries. The young, the underprivileged and the maladjusted are still vulnerable and may need help but the idea of women forced into prostitution to avoid destitution is no longer tenable in the Western world. Unfortunately, the old idea that gullible girls can be tricked by 'white slavers' into believing that they are being offered well-paid dancing engagements abroad is all too true today. Much of Sean O'Callaghan's account of his personal investigations in his book, *The White Slave Trade*,[11] describing how girls are transported to the Middle East and there kept dependent through drug addiction, may be checked through other sources. It is no use pretending that teenage girls who have run away from home or who, for some reason or other, are on their own, are a match for the representatives of large-scale international agencies, which have organized prostitution on a commercial basis.

The tendency of governments in most Western countries is to try to check the commercial exploitation of vice and the 'scandal' of solicitation in the streets, leaving prostitution as a private enterprise occupation and, in some instances, as in Hamburg, providing limited facilities for it. The former objective has resulted in legislation such as the Sexual Offences Act 1956 (4 and 5 Eliz. 2) in this country, imposing relatively severe penalties for men living on the earnings of prostitutes and women exercising control over prostitutes. The latter objective resulted in the Street Offences Act of 1959 (7 and 8 Eliz. 2) increasing the penalties for soliciting in the streets, particularly for cumulative offences. Exception was taken by the feminists to this latter act as applying to women and not to men and for the continuation of special legislation applying to the 'common prostitute' – a term which, it is maintained, should be banished from the statute book. This, one may think, is fair enough, and simply a continuation of the policy of opposing double moral standards.

Perhaps conventional thought has underestimated the number of women who dislike a regular, not to say monotonous, life. Though most of these women stick it out, so to speak, we hear of captive wives and housebound mothers, as well as loose women. The situation has to be faced, in contrast to earlier beliefs, that there are women who are prepared to act as prostitutes in spite of the fact that they would not otherwise become destitute, and that there is likely to be a continuing demand for their services, even though marital adjustment may become easier and affectional relationships outside marriage more easily come by. There will always be men who do not wish to be under any obligation other than a financial one, as well as the footloose, the deviants and the unattractive. It is being increasingly realized that the study of the prostitute cannot be divorced from that of her customer and the Josephine Butler Society made a contribution towards this by providing facilities, in 1962, for the annual Alison Neilans Memorial Lecture to be on the subject of 'The Clients of Prostitutes.'[12] One of the interesting ideas put forward by Dr Gibbens in this lecture was that the well-established image of the prostitute as the safety-valve of marriage may be ill founded. A series of men at a V.D. clinic was interviewed and most of the men who admitted to having been with prostitutes said their marriages were satisfactory (though there appears to be some doubt if this assessment was entirely accurate). The interviewers had expected the men to say that they were misunderstood or unhappily married and were considerably surprised.[13] On examination, both the prostitute and her client seem pathetic figures in comparison with the commercial elements that exploit them.

The objects of the Josephine Butler Society today are the same as those of its founder, namely, opposition to the state regulation of prostitution and to traffic in persons. While the Society, like Mrs

Butler, does not think that prostitution should be made a legal offence, it is still basically 'against sin' and is not in sympathy with the idea that prostitution should be looked upon as a necessary trade or social service. Although the idea is not new, the belief seems to be gaining ground in some circles today that if prostitution can be looked upon as a necessary trade, it is unjust for the trader to be ostracized.

Perhaps the only valid contribution the historian can make to this complex subject is to emphasize the transitory nature of fashionable explanations for social phenomena. We have seen the prostitute viewed as a 'fallen woman', as the victim of economic circumstances, as a psychologically maladjusted individual and as someone who likes easy money and dislikes an orderly life. To some extent the wheel is turning full circle, for the idea of someone voluntarily choosing prostitution rather than 'honest work' is nearer that of the Victorian 'fallen woman' than to some of the intervening images, including the literary image of the tarnished woman who nevertheless is warm-hearted and basically generous and good. Who is to say that, in another decade, today's image will not be superseded?

It has been seen that family planning did not become a major feminist objective until after the First World War, when a fair amount of feminist support was given to outstanding women such as Marie Stopes and Margaret Sanger. In the present-day context, it is sometimes maintained that the provision of family planning services is of less importance to family limitation than a high standard of living. Once there is the determination to maintain living standards through limiting family size, relatively old-fashioned methods, or techniques as old as time, will suffice.

The liberalization of the law relating to abortion which took place in Britain in 1968 owes even less to feminist support than does family planning, women's organizations being divided on the issue and those with religious connections, such as the Mothers' Union, understandably opposing easier abortion. Of course, both family planning and the termination of pregnancy for social as well as medical reasons can easily be supported on humanitarian grounds, but it seems odd that no group of feminists (so far as the writer knows) has come out with the forthright claim that it should be an essential aspect of freedom of person for a woman to refuse to have an unwanted child.

The new woman of the 'nineties who chose free love was not really a success and lacked influence. She needed to be childless and to live in Bohemian circles to have anything like a satisfactory life. She was not, of course, particularly new, as a reference back to the life of Georges Sand shows.

We have noticed that the feminist movement has been accused of bringing in piecemeal reform and of concentrating on civil rights, particularly the vote, while ignoring the personal and sexua freedom of women. Undoubtedly the main body of feminists concentrated on civil rights and particularly on the attainment of the franchise, as the parliamentary vote proved their most intractable obstacle. Also, when moral matters were not shunned altogether, there was a concentration on high rather than liberal moral standards. This does not mean, however, that feminist successes would have been greater and speedier if there had been pressure for greater sexual tolerance and a more liberal moral climate. The anti-feminists always maintained that freedom for women would lead to licence, moral degradation, and so on and it was only by the reassuring respectability of those involved that the first steps for the improved education of women and girls were successfully taken. It has been seen that in America the connection between the feminists and Victoria Woodhull, who was involved in a public scandal and associated with free love, proved a setback to the movement. Dr Richard Marsden Pankhurst's contention that any breach of sexual morality attracted so much attention that it was impossible for those concerned to have influence in other directions was broadly justified and it was doubtful if the feminists (a minority in the community, like all pressure groups) would have gained the successes they did if their morals had not been impeccable. The militant suffragettes made a unique, though largely unintended, contribution towards the liberalization of moral standards through their challenge to convention generally. After their window-smashing, arson and other 'outrages', the stereotype of woman as a docile, dependent creature could no longer be maintained. Freedom cannot be kept in separate compartments and although it may be more difficult to change traditional ways of thinking than legal rights, the two must interact. In the main, however, the sexual revolution of our time has resulted from the breaking of the link between sex and consequential pregnancy and the loosening of the age-old association between sex and guilt, the association of feminism with these developments being minimal.

A partial answer only can be given to the question, posed in the first chapter, of whether a woman is judged and valued on the basis of her 'respectability' and little else. It seems to depend very much on where she lives and her social circle. Obviously, the rich and successful in the entertainment world can do more or less as they please and society generally is less censorious than it used to be. Equally obviously, there are considerable areas of society in which the old standards of judgment prevail. There are, perhaps, generation gaps and also regional differences. We talk a lot about sex equality but this ideal seems to have found greater acceptance in the south of England than elsewhere in Britain. On August 7th, 1968, *The Times* printed an interview with the Scots tycoon, Sir Hugh Fraser, in which he said, 'I must admit that I am changing my attitude [to women] a bit. Now my wife goes out once a fortnight to play bridge in the evening: four years ago I wouldn't have dreamed of allowing that.'[14] The fact is that while a wife's responsibility for home affairs is still looked upon as essential to her role as a good wife, a wide variety of roles is permitted to the husband within the home, from extreme helpfulness to uselessness, and from that of partner to 'boss', without him being looked upon as a bad husband. (The obverse side of the coin, of course, is that the husband is expected to work and bring money into the home but his wife is allowed a choice in this respect without forfeiting social approval.)

It is understandable that there has been a very limited campaign for a freedom which relatively few women seem to want. The ideal is still the happy marriage rather than sexual freedom and the complaints made by both feminists and non-feminists are mainly directed against the obstacles which marriage puts in the way of activities other than domestic, that is to say the practical difficulties and worry involved in running a home and a job. As Hannah Mitchell continually emphasized in her book, *The Hard Way Up*,[15] the work of the world cannot be done between meals. Barbara

Castle put her finger on the sore spot when she commented, while Minister of Transport, 'It doesn't matter who you are, at the back of a woman's life there is always some thought like, "My God, it's Friday and I've forgotten the laundry." '[16]

The history of feminism and, indeed, the development of public morality would have been very different if men and women had not fallen in love without reference to the conventional moral standards and then turned, as a consequence, to question and examine the standards or to take up a cause which their partner held dear. Trapped in conventional morality and influenced by Harriet Taylor, John Stuart Mill placed the prestige of his intellect behind the feminist cause and produced the book which was practically to become the feminist bible, *The Subjection of Women*. William Thompson's earlier *Appeal* of 1825 had resulted from his admiration for Anna Wheeler and the combined decision of Annie Besant and Charles Bradlaugh (who would have married if they could) to stand trial on the issue of their right to disseminate knowledge of birth control was much more effective than if either had acted alone. Marie Stopes's unsatisfactory marriage directed her thoughts towards the idea that men and women had a right to find both love and sexual satisfaction in marriage. To take love in its wider sense, it was Josephine Butler's all-embracing love for humanity but particularly for outcast women which was the motive force behind her campaign, combined, of course, with a very proper feeling for constitutional rights.

It may be felt that this review of the interaction of love, morality and feminism has been somewhat indeterminate, but in a period when the social role of women is being increasingly examined, it is surely unsatisfactory if little attempt is made to balance the many accounts of the campaigns for the vote and civil rights with some review of the extent to which women have escaped from the cramping restraints of the Victorian interpretation of morality. The emancipation of women depends as much on social attitudes as legal rights, although the two interact. In so far as women have escaped from the straitjacket of Victorian morality one wants to learn to what extent this is the result of their own efforts or whether the feminists have simply kept pace with, or even lagged behind, the general moral climate. One can only conclude that while advocates of a more liberal moral climate have tended to be feminist, the feminist movement has not been in the vanguard. The attitude held has been perfectly expressed by Dame Margery Corbett Ashby, writing as recently as December 1968. In reviewing '50 Years of Woman Suffrage', she states:

> In one respect we have been disappointed. When we urged an equal moral standard we thought to raise men's standard of sex conduct and moral responsibility to that previously expected of women. Now it seems that an equal moral standard means equal promiscuity for both sexes.[17]

Dame Margery is an admired and respected figure in her eighties and while she may not typify the generality of present-day feminists, she is certainly typical of her generation.

To sum up, the impact of feminism upon morality has not been negligible. There has been consistent and persistent pressure for equal moral standards; no coherent, feminist attitude towards the morality of the Divorce Laws has emerged; there was a successful campaign, led by Josephine Butler, against the Contagious Diseases Acts, followed by an international movement against the state regulation of vice; widespread feminist support has been given to the United Nations in its efforts towards the suppression of the traffic in women and girls; in France and Italy, the closing of brothels in 1945 and 1962 respectively was largely the result of the activities of two outstanding women, Mme Marthe Richard and Senator Signorina Angeline Merlin; feminist recognition of family planning was somewhat belated but a fair amount of support was eventually given; feminist pressure for easier abortion has been negligible; in the Anglo-Saxon countries, the mainstream of the feminist movement has supported conventional moral standards, hoping that men's morals would be raised to those of respectable women and that 'high and equal moral standards' would be attained by all levels of society.

Notes

1 McGregor, O. R., 'Take This Woman – A Look at Marriage and Divorce in 1968', in *Evening Standard*, 20 March 1968, 8, col. 2.
2 Comfort, Alex, *Sex in Society*, 1963, 16.

3 Cf. Fletcher, Ronald, *The Family and Marriage in Britain*, 1966.

4 H.L. Deb., 5S, Vol. 286, cc. 426–8.

5 *The Times*, 18.12.1968, 1, col. 1.

6 *Ibid.*, 14, col. 4.

7 *The Times*, 7.12.1968, 4, col. 6.

8 *Ibid*, col. 7.

9 H.L. Deb., 5S, Vol. 286, c. 427.

10 Cf. *Report of the XXIst Triennial Congress*, 1967, 37. (Pubd. 1967 by the I.A.W.)

11 O'Callaghan, Sean, *The White Slave Trade*, 1965.

12 Gibbens, T. C. N., 'The Clients of Prostitutes', lecture delivered on 29.11.1962, reproduced as a pamphlet by the Josephine Butler Society.

13 *Ibid.*, 10–11.

14 *Op. cit.*, p. 7, c. 4. No. 3 of Stella King's series, 'Men Talking About Women', in *The Times*, 7.8.1968.

15 Mitchell, Hannah, *The Hard Way Up*, 1968.

16 Quoted in 'Britain 1968, Women Talking', the *Observer*, colour supplement, 28.1.1968.

17 Ashby, Dame Margery Corbett, '50 Years of Woman Suffrage', in *The Shield*, 1968, 16.

Bibliography

Books, pamphlets (p) and articles (a), published in London unless otherwise stated.

Public Documents

Acts of Parliament:

> Matrimonial Causes Act, 1857
> Contagious Diseases Acts of 1864, 1866 and 1869
> Criminal Law Amendment Act, 1885
> Sexual Offences Act, 1956
> Street Offences Act, 1959
> Abortion Act, 1967.
> Maintenance Orders Act, 1968
> Divorce Reform Act, 1969

H.C. Bills:

> Divorce Reform Bill, 1967 (18)
> Divorce Reform Bill, 1968 (17)
> Matrimonial Property Bill, 1968 (23).

Papal Encyclical: *Humanae Vitae.*

Parliamentary Debates:
> 3rd Series Hansard's Parliamentary Debates
> 4th Series Parliamentary Debates (Authorized)
> 5th Series Parliamentary Debates (Official).

Books, pamphlets (p) and articles (a), published in London unless otherwise stated.

Reports:

Select Committee of the House of Lords on the Contagious Diseases Act, 1866, H.L. Parliamentary Papers 1867–8 (113)

Royal Commission on the Contagious Diseases Acts, 1871; C. 408 and 408–1

Select Committee of the House of Commons on the Contagious Diseases Acts, 1879–1881; C. 323, 1879; C. 114, 1880; C. 308, Sess. 2, 1880; C. 351, 1881; C. 340, 1882

Select Committee of the House of Lords to inquire into the state of the Law relative to the PROTECTION OF YOUNG GIRLS from Artifices to induce them to lead a Corrupt Life, and into the means of Amending the same, 1882; H.L. Parliamentary Papers 1881 (145) and 1882 (188)

Royal Commission on Population, 1949, Cmd. 8695

Royal Commission on Marriage and Divorce, 1951–55, Cmd. 9678

Committee on Homosexual Offences and Prostitution, 1957 (Wolfenden Report), Cmnd. 247

Study on Traffic in Persons and Prostitution. United Nations, Department of Economic and Social Affairs, New York, 1959.

Books, Pamphlets and Articles

ACLAND, Alice, *Caroline Norton*, Constable, 1948.

ACTON, William, *Prostitution considered in its Moral, Social and Sanitary Aspects, etc.*, 1857.

ALLAN, Grant, *The Woman Who Did*, 1895.

ANON, *Streetwalker*, Bodley Head, 1959.

ARNSTEIN, Walter L., *The Bradlaugh Case*, Clarendon Press, Oxford, 1965.

BANKS, J. A. and Olive, *Prosperity and Parenthood*, Routledge and Kegan Paul, 1954.

—— *Feminism and Family Planning in Victorian England*, Liverpool University Press, 1964.

BAX, E. Belfort, *The Fraud of Feminism*, Grant Richards, 1913.

BEAUVOIR, Simone de, *The Second Sex*, Jonathan Cape, 1953.

—— *The Marquis de Sade*, John Collins, 1962.

Books, pamphlets (p) and articles (a), published in London unless otherwise stated.

BELL, E. Moberley, *Josephine Butler*, Constable, 1962.

BESANT, Annie, (p) *The Political Status of Women* (3rd ed.), 1874.

—— (p) *The Law of Population*, 1877.

—— *An Autobiography* (3rd ed.), 1893.

BESTERMAN, Theodore, *Mrs Annie Besant*, Kegan Paul, 1934.

BODICHON, Barbara, (p) *A Brief Summary in Plain Language of the Most Important Laws Concerning Women*, 1855.

BOUTEN, Dr J., *Mary Wollstonecraft and the Beginning of Female Emancipation in England and France*, Amsterdam, 1923.

BOX, Muriel, *The Trial of Marie Stopes*, Femina Books, 1967.

BRAILSFORD, H. N., *Shelley, Godwin and Their Circle*, Oxford University Press, 1951. (1st ed. 1913.)

BREED, Mary, *See* How-Martyn.

BRENTON, Myron, *The American Male*, Allen & Unwin, 1967.

BRIANT, Keith, *Marie Stopes*, Hogarth Press, 1962.

BUTLER, A. S. G., *Portrait of Josephine Butler*, Faber & Faber, 1954.

BUTLER, E. M., *The Saint-Simonian Religion in Germany*, Cambridge University Press, 1926.

BUTLER, Josephine E., (p) *The Constitution Violated*, Edinburgh, 1871.

—— (p) *The New Abolitionists*, 1876.

—— *Rebecca Jarrett*, 1885.

—— *Personal Reminiscences of a Great Crusade*, 1896.

CAMPBELL, Rev R. J., (p) *Women's Suffrage and the Social Evil*, Women's Freedom League, 1907.

CLARK, G. Kitson, *The Making of Victorian England*, Methuen, 1962.

CLAYTON, Joseph, *Robert Owen, Social Pioneer*, Firfield, 1908.

CLEPHANE, Irene, *Towards Sex Freedom*, Bodley Head, 1935.

COLE, G. D. H., (p) *Richard Carlile*, Fabian Society, 1943.

COLE, Margaret, *Robert Owen*, Bletchworth Press, 1953.

COMFORT, Alex, *Sex in Society*, Duckworth, 1963.

COMINOS, Peter, (a) 'Late Victorian Sexual Respectability and the Social System', in *International Review of Social History*, viii, 1963.

Books, pamphlets (p) and articles (a), published in London unless
otherwise stated.

CONDORCET, Marquis de, (p) *Sur l'admission des femmes au droit de
Cité*, 1790. Translated by Dr Alice Drysdale Vickery, Letchworth
Garden City Press (N.D.).

CROMPTON, Margaret, *George Eliot: The Woman*, Cassell, 1960.

DAHLSTROM, Edmund (ed.), *The Changing Roles of Men and Women*,
Duckworth, 1962.

DANGERFIELD, George, *The Strange Death of Liberal England*,
Constable, 1936.

DEACON, Richard, *The Private Life of Mr Gladstone*, Frederick
Muller, 1965.

DEVEY, Louisa, *Life of Rosina, Lady Lytton*, 1887.

DEVLIN, Patrick, *The Enforcement of Morals*, Oxford University
Press, 1965.

DITZION, Sidney, *Marriage, Morals and Sex in America*, New York,
1953.

DRINNON, Richard, *Rebel in Paradise: A Biography of Emma Goldman*, University of Chicago, 1961.

DRYSDALE, G. R., *Elements of Social Science*, 1854.

FAWCETT, Mrs Henry (Dame Millicent), *Introduction* to 1891 edition
of Mary Wollstonecraft's *Vindication of the Rights of Woman*.

FERNANDO, Lloyd, (a) 'The Radical Ideology of the New Woman',
in *Southern Review*, ii, no. 3, 1967.

FLETCHER, Ronald, *The Family and Marriage in Britain*, Pelican, 1966.

FRIEDAN, Betty, *The Feminine Mystique*, Penguin Books, 1965.

FRIENDS' ABOLITIONIST ASSOCIATION, (p) *The Spiritual Side of
the Life-Work of Josephine Butler*, 1908.

FRÖLICH, Paul, *Rosa Luxemburg*, Victor Gollancz, 1940.

FRYER, Peter, *Mrs Grundy: Studies in English Prudery*, Dennis Dob-
son, 1963.

—— *The Birth Controllers*, Secker & Warburg, 1965.

FYFE, Hamilton, *Revolt of Women*, Rich & Cowan, 1933.

GARNETT, Richard, *The Life of W. J. Fox*, Bodley Head, 1910.

GATTEY, Charles Neilson, *The Bloomer Girls*, Femina Books, 1967.

GIBBENS, T. C. N., (p) *The Clients of Prostitutes*, Josephine Butler
Society, 1962.

Books, pamphlets (p) and articles (a), published in London unless otherwise stated.

GODWIN, William, *Memoirs of Mary Wollstonecraft*, 1798.

—— *Thoughts on Man*, 1831.

GOODWIN, Michael (ed.), *Nineteenth Century Opinion*, Pelican, 1951.

GORER, Geoffrey, *The Life and Ideas of the Marquis de Sade*, Peter Owen, 1953.

GRIMES, Alan P., *The Puritan Ethic and Woman Suffrage*, Oxford University Press, 1967.

GRISEWOOD, F. (ed.), *Ideas and Beliefs of the Victorians*, 1949.

HAIGHT, Gordon S., *George Eliot: A Biography*, Clarendon Press, Oxford, 1968.

HALÉVY, Elie, *A History of the English People in the 19th Century*, Benn, 1952.

HAMMOND, J. L. and Barbara, *James Stanfeld – A Victorian Champion of Sex Equality*, Longmans, 1932.

HANCOCK, Edward, *Robert Owen's Community System, etc., and the Horrid Doings of the St Simonians*, 1832.

HAY-COOPER, L., *Josephine Butler*, S.P.C.K., 1922.

HAYEK, F. A., *John Stuart Mill and Harriet Taylor*, Routledge & Kegan Paul, 1951.

HENRIQUES, Fernando, *Prostitution and Society* (3 vols.), MacGibbon & Kee, 1963.

HOLMES, Marion, (p) *Josephine Butler*, Women's Freedom League (N.D.).

HOUSMAN, Laurence, (p) *The Immoral Effect of Ignorance in Sex Relations*, Women's Freedom League, 1911.

—— (p) *The Sex War and Women's Suffrage*, Women's Freedom League, 1912.

HOW-MARTYN, Edith and BREED, Mary, (p) *The Birth Control Movement in England*, John Bale, Sons & Dowelson, 1930.

HUNT, Morton M., *The Natural History of Love*, Alfred A. Knopf, New York, 1959.

—— *Her Infinite Variety*, Harper & Row, New York, 1962.

INGLIS, Brian, *Private Conscience, Public Morality*, André Deutsch, 1964.

JOAD, C. E. M., (p) *Robert Owen, Idealist*, Fabian Tract 182, 1928.

Books, pamphlets (p) and articles (a), published in London unless otherwise stated.

JOHNSON, G. W., *The Evolution of Women*, Robt. Holden, 1926.

JOHNSON, George W. and Lucy A. (eds.), *Josephine Butler: An Autobiographical Memoir*, Arrowsmith, Bristol, 1913.

JOHNSTON, Johanna, *Mrs Satan*, Macmillan, 1967.

KAMM, Josephine, *Rapiers and Battleaxes*, Allen & Unwin, 1966.

KEGAN PAUL, C., *William Godwin, His Friends and Contemporaries*, 1876.

KEY, Ellen, *Love and Marriage*, G. P. Putnam, New York, 1911.

KLEIN, Viola, *Feminine Character*, Routledge & Kegan Paul, 1946.

KNOWLTON, Charles, *Fruits of Philosophy*, U.S.A., 1832.

LEACH, Edmund, (a) Reith Lectures, 1967, printed in *The Listener*, particularly the issue of 7 December, 1967.

LECKY, W. E. H., *History of European Morals*, 1869.

LEIGH SMITH, Barbara. *See* Bodichon.

LOGAN, William, *The Great Social Evil*, Hodder & Stoughton, 1871.

LONGFORD, Elizabeth, *Victoria R.I.*, Pan Books, 1964.

MCGREGOR, O. R., *Divorce in England: a Centenary Study*, Heinemann, 1957. (a) Series in the *Evening Standard* 'I Take This Woman', March 18th, 1968, *et seq.*

MARCUS, Steven, *The Other Victorians*, Weidenfeld & Nicolson, 1966.

MARTIN, Sir Theodore, *Queen Victoria as I Knew Her*, Blackwood, 1908.

MILL, Harriet, Mrs John Stuart Mill, (a) 'The Enfranchisement of Women', in *Westminster Review*, 1851.

MILL, James (a) 'Government', *Encyclopaedia Britannica*, Supplement to 4th (1824) Edition.

MILL, John Stuart, *Subjection of Women*, 1869.

—— *Autobiography*, 1873.

MINEKA, Francis E., *The Dissidence of Dissent*, Chapel Hill, University of North Carolina, 1944.

MITCHELL, David, *The Fighting Pankhursts*, Jonathan Cape, 1967.

MITCHELL, Hannah, *The Hard Way Up*, Faber & Faber, 1968.

MORRIS, Desmond, *The Naked Ape*, Jonathan Cape, 1967.

174　*Bibliography*

Books, pamphlets (p) and articles (a), published in London unless otherwise stated.

NETHERCOT, A. H., *The First Five Lives of Annie Besant*, Rupert Hart-Davis, 1961. (First published Chicago, 1960.)

——— *The Last Four Lives of Annie Besant*, Rupert Hart-Davis, 1963.

NETTL, J. P., *Life of Rosa Luxemburg*, Oxford University Press, 1966.

NICHOLSON, Max, *The System*, Hodder & Stoughton, 1967.

O'CALLAGHAN, Sean, *The White Slave Trade*, Robert Hale, 1965.

OWEN, Robert, *Book of the New Moral World*, 1836.

——— *The Life of Robert Owen*, 1857.

OWEN, Robert Dale, *Moral Physiology: or a Brief and Plain Treatise on the Population Question*, New York, 1831.

——— *Threading My Way*, New York, 1874.

PACKE, Michael St John, *The Life of John Stuart Mill*, Secker & Warburg, 1954.

PANKHURST, Christabel, *The Great Scourge and How to End It*, E. Pankhurst, 1913.

PANKHURST, R. K. P., (a) 'Saint-Simonism in England', in *The Twentieth Century*, Dec. 1952 and Jan. 1953.

——— *William Thompson*, Watts, 1954.

PETHICK LAWRENCE, F. W., *Fate Has Been Kind*, Hutchinson, 1943.

PIKE, E. Royston, *Human Documents of the Victorian Golden Age*, Allen & Unwin, 1967.

PODMORE, Frank, *Robert Owen, A Biography*, 1906.

RAYMOND, John (ed.), *Queen Victoria's Early Letters*, Batsford, 1963.

ROBERTSON, J. M., *Pioneer Humanists*, Watts, 1907.

ROVER, Constance, *Women's Suffrage and Party Politics in Britain, 1866–1914*, Routledge & Kegan Paul, 1967.

——— *The Punch Book of Women's Rights*, Hutchinson, 1967.

RUSSELL, Bertrand, *Autobiography: Vol. I 1872–1914*, Allen & Unwin, 1967.

SADE, Marquis de, *Justine*, 1791.

——— *Juliette*, 1792.

——— *La Philosophie dans le Boudoir*, 1795.

SADLIER, Michael, *Bulwer Lytton and His Wife*, Constable, 1933.

SAINT-SIMON, Claude-Henri de Rouvroy, Comte de, *Nouveau Christianisme*, 1825.

Books, pamphlets (p) and articles (a), published in London unless otherwise stated.

SAND, Georges, *Indiana*, 1832.

—— *Lélia*, 1833.

SANGER, Margaret, (p) *Family Limitation, circa* 1914.

SANGER, William, *History of Prostitution, its Extent, Causes and Effects throughout the World*, New York, 1919.

SCHUR, Edwin M. (ed.), *The Family and The Sexual Revolution*, Allen & Unwin, 1964.

SHAPLEN, Robert, *Free Love and Heavenly Sinners*, André Deutsch, 1956.

SINCLAIR, Andrew, *The Better Half*, Jonathan Cape, 1966.

SNOWDON, Ethel, *The Feminist Movement*, Collins, 1913.

STAFFORD, Ann, *The Age of Consent*, Hodder & Stoughton, 1964.

STEAD, W. T., (a) 'Maiden Tribute to Modern Babylon' Series in *Pall Mall Gazette*, July 6th, 1885, *et seq.*

—— *Josephine Butler, a Life Sketch*, Morgan & Scott, 1887.

STEPHENS, Winifred, *Women of the French Revolution*, Chapman & Hall, 1922.

STOPES, Marie Carmichael, *Married Love*, A. C. Firfield, 1918.

—— *Wise Parenthood*, A. C. Firfield, 1918.

—— *Contraception: Birth Control, Its Theory, History and Practice*, J. Bole, 1923.

STRACHEY, Ray, *The Cause*, G. Bell, 1928.

—— *Millicent Garrett Fawcett*, John Murray, 1931.

SUTHERLAND, Dr Halliday, (p) *Birth Control: A Statement of Christian Doctrine against the Neo-Malthusians*, 1922.

THOMPSON, William, *Appeal of One-Half of the Human Race, Women, against the Pretensions of the Other Half, Men, to Restrain them in Political and thence in Civil and Domestic Slavery*, 1825.

TURNER, E. M., (p) *Josephine Butler: Her Place in History*, The Association for Moral and Social Hygiene (N.D.).

UNSWORTH, Madge, *Maiden Tribute*, Salvationist Publishing, 1949.

WARDLE, R. M., *Mary Wollstonecraft*, University of Kansas Press, 1951.

WEST, Geoffrey, *Mrs Annie Besant*, Gerald Howe, 1927.

WEST, Rebecca, 'Mrs Pankhurst', an essay in *The Post Victorians*, Nicholson & Watson, 1933.

WESTERMARCK, E. A., *History of Human Marriage*, 1891.

—— *The Origin and Development of Moral Ideas*, 1906–8.

Books, pamphlets (p) and articles (a), published in London unless otherwise stated.

WINWAR, Frances, *The Life of the Heart: Georges Sand and Her Times*, Hamish Hamilton, 1946.

WOLLSTONECRAFT, Mary, *Thoughts on the Education of Daughters*, 1787.

—— *Vindication of the Rights of Woman*, 1792.

—— *Letters to Imlay*, 1879.

WRIGHT, Sir Almroth E., *The Unexpurgated Case Against Woman Suffrage*, Constable, 1913.

YOUNG, G. M., *Victorian England*, Oxford University Press, 1960.

Manuscript

Josephine Butler letters, Fawcett Library (incorporating Josephine Butler Library)

Unpublished Thesis

SAYWELL, R., 'The Development of Feminist Ideas in England, 1789–1833', M.A. Thesis, University of London, 1936.

Newspapers and Periodicals

Published in Britain, unless otherwise indicated

The Adult
Birth Control Review (U.S.A.)
Black Dwarf (*circa* 1818)
Crisis
Deist
The Economist
Englishwoman
Englishwoman's Journal
Englishwoman's Review
Evening Standard
Fortnightly Review
Fraser's Magazine
Globe
Guardian
Guy's Hospital Gazette
Isis
Listener

Monthly Repository
National Reformer
Observer
Pall Mall Gazette
Political Register
Punch
Reformer
Republican
Shield
Suffragette
Sunday Times
The Times
Twentieth Century
Victoria Magazine
Westminster Review
Woman Rebel (U.S.A.)
Women Speaking (U.K. and Canada)

Index

Economist, The, 48-9
Edward VII, 111
Egerton, George, 132
Elements of Social Science, 133-4
Eliot, George, 24
Ellis, Havelock, 68, 70, 137
Encyclopaedia Britannica, 38
Enfantin, Barthélémy Prosper, 10
Enfranchisement of Women, 38
Englishwoman's Review, 105
Era of Theodore Roosevelt, 57
Essay on Population, 100
Every Woman's Book, 23
Exeter, Bishop of, 58, 69

Family and Marriage in Britain, 167
Family and the Sexual Revolution, 152
Family planning, see Birth control
Family Planning Act (1967), 121
Family Planning Association, 118
Fate Has Been Kind, 6
Fawcett, Dame Millicent, 45, 48,
    52-5, 57, 84, 105, 120, 143-4,
    148
  Henry, 104-5
Fawcett Society, 18
Feminine Mystique, The, 130
Feminism and Family Planning in
    Victorian England, 6, 101, 109, 145
Femme Libre, La, 27
Fighting Pankhursts, The, 152
First Five Lives of Annie Besant, 102,
    109
Fletcher, Ronald, 167
Flower, Eliza, 31-4
  Sarah, 31-2
Foote, Dr, 128
Fox, Mrs, 32-3
  William Johnson, 31-5, 38, 40
France, feminism in, 7-12
Frankenstein, 17
Fraser, Sir Hugh, 164, 167
Free Enquirer, The, 127
Free love, 1, 7-12, 55
Free Love and Heavenly Sinners, 130
Freethought, 22
French Revolution, 1, 7-13, 16
Friedan, Mrs Betty, 130
Fruits of Philosophy, 101, 104, 127

Fryer, Peter, 101
Fujii Kuyiro, 117
Fuseli, 14

'Gagging' Acts, 20
Garnett, Richard, 34, 40
Garrett, Elizabeth, see Garrett Ander-
    son, Dr Elizabeth
Garrett, Millicent, see Fawcett, Dame
    Millicent
Garrett Anderson, Dr Elizabeth, 52,
    81
Gates, Dr R. G., 111-12, 118
Gatty, C. N., 101
Gerald, Queenie, 142-3
Gibbens, Dr T. C. N., 161, 167
Gladstone, W. E., 81, 100
Glover, Edward, 65
Godwin, Mary, 16-17
  William, 15-19
Goldman, Emma, 2, 6, 128, 129, 131
    134-5, 153
Goulden, Emmeline, see Pankhurst
    Mrs Emmeline
Great Scourge and How to End It, The
    143, 152
Great Social Evil, The, 70
Grimes, Alan, 49, 57

Hancock, Edward, 26, 30
Harcourt, Sir William, 87
Hard Way Up, The, 164, 167
Hardie, Keir, 69, 143
Harewood case, 44
Harman, Moses, 128
Hastings, G. W., 87-8
Hay-Cooper, L., 131, 152
Hayek, F. A., 39, 40
Heath, Edward, 150
Henriques, Dr Fernando, 68, 70, 96
Herbert, Sidney, 29
Hewlett, Maurice, 117
History of European Morals, 67, 70
History of Prostitution, 125, 129, 130
Hone, William, 21
Hooker, Isabell a Beecher, 124
Hopwood, C. H., 87
Housman, Laurence, 111, 114-15, 121
How-Martyn, Edith, 120, 129